The Best Places to Bed & Breakfast

A Selective Guide

Fifth Edition

Janette Higgins

Illustrations by Audrey Caryi, Jane James and Mark Pettes
Cover watercolour by Elizabeth Berry

*Carol & Brian
Happy Trails
Janette Higgins*

JUNO PRESS

The Best Places to Bed & Breakfast in Ontario
A Selective Guide
Fifth edition

Juno Press P.O. Box 502
Port Hope, ON, Canada L1A 3Z4

Trade distribution by: Firefly Books, 3680 Victoria Park Ave
Toronto, ON, Canada M2H 3K1

Printed and bound in Canada

Canadian Cataloguing in Publication Data

The National Library of Canada has catalogued this publication as follows:

Higgins, Janette, date
     The Best Places to B&B in Ontario

[1988] –
Some issues have title: The best places to bed and breakfast
in Ontario.
ISSN 0841-6184
ISBN 0-921516-04-5 (5th ed.)

I. Bed and breakfast accommodations – Ontario
– Directories.   I. Title.   II. Title: Best places to B&B in
Ontario, III. Title: Best places to bed & breakfast in Ontario,
IV. Title: Best places to bed & breakfast in Ontario.

TX910.C2H53   647'.94713   C88-031809-0 rev

Acknowledgements

This book is self-published. Which means I do the research, writing, publishing and some marketing. Along the way, though, I get *considerable* help.

Kudos to Audrey Caryi, of Warkworth, and Jane James, of Bowmanville, who sketched most of the nostalgic illustrations; and to Jane's brother, Mark Pettes, who pitched in to do the rest; to Elizabeth Berry, of Toronto, who painted the evocative watercolour on the cover; and to Steven Bock of the Toronto firm, Public Good, for his graphic design expertise.

Appreciation to friends, family and editor: you each, in your own way, make a contribution to this enterprise. Sometimes more than you know.

And a special thanks to Adrienne Clarkson – without her encouragement to continue, you wouldn't be holding this edition of the book.

Janette Higgins

How This Book Came To Be

Here's what some of the headings mean:

Season: B&Bs open "all year" *may* be closed occasionally – hosts need holidays too.

Rates: are for 1998, and applicable taxes are indicated. PST is 5%. GST is 7%.

Restrictions: if children, smoking or guests' pets are NOT allowed, it's noted here.

In residence: for those with allergies or aversions, I've noted pets, smokers or children in the B&B. Some pets are kept away from guests and some give an exuberant welcome. Most host smokers are discreet.

Breakfast: continental usually includes fruit or juice, cold cereals, breads or muffins, coffee or tea, and sometimes cheese, yogurt or a boiled egg. Full includes bacon and eggs, or some other cooked dish like pancakes or quiche.

When I first wrote this book, I did it because I couldn't find a B&B guide that wasn't paid advertising written by hosts. I wanted to give accurate and perceptive assessments of Ontario's best B&Bs. So I travelled incognito to several hundred, paid where I stayed, and picked those that excelled. To remain independent, I didn't charge hosts. Great for consumers. They could trust the book. And great for hosts, who got a lot of extra business because of it.

But not so great for me. I *did* sell a respectable number of books. But after three years, I was only making minimum wage. Since I didn't leave my management job to live at the poverty level, what to do. I didn't think I could increase sales that much. I *could* charge more – but $30 is a lot to pay for this book. Or I could give it up and get a *real* job.

The only viable option was to charge hosts. But how to stay reasonably independ-ent. I decided to *still* travel incognito, pay for stays, and select the best. The *only* difference would be that hosts would pay a modest participation fee.

You might wonder if hosts now have control over the stories, as for advertising. They don't. I make it clear that what I write is not an ad; it's still my opinion. If hosts don't accept this, I'm prepared to refund their fee. Most important, *no one can buy their way into this book*.

So I can't honestly call my book inde-pendent any more – the operative word is *selective*. I'm still *very* picky.

Janette Higgins

B&B Etiquette

Things are sometimes a little different when you're staying in a B&B home, rather than an inn or hotel. Here are some tips to ease the transition:

- If you have special dietary requirements, ask whether they can be accommodated when you book.
- Ask about cancellation and refund policies when you book.
- Let your hosts know when you plan to arrive and *call if it changes*. Hosts plan their schedules around your arrival time.
- If you don't have a reservation, try to phone before dropping in.
- Knock, don't just walk in the front door as I've seen some people do.
- Remember you're paying for bed and breakfast. Plan to arrive no earlier than late afternoon, and to leave by mid-morning.
- Hosts need their privacy. Respect private areas of the home.
- If you're sharing a bathroom you'll have to speed up your toilette – aim for 10-15 minutes.
- Keep showers short – there's not always a lot of hot water.
- Don't leave personal articles or towels behind in a shared bathroom (neither should your hosts).
- Don't expect babysitting, laundry facilities or room in the fridge. Treat it as a bonus if you get it.
- Show up for breakfast at the agreed-upon time.
- Introduce yourself to the other guests if your host is busy.
- If you're staying more than one night, be aware that some hosts don't make beds because they feel like they're intruding on *your* private space. So if you want your bed made up and towels changed, let them know.
- Relax and enjoy what each B&B has to offer. You're a welcome guest in someone's home, and your hosts are in the business because they enjoy the stimulation of interesting, warm and friendly people. Just like yourself.

Contents

HEADING NORTH

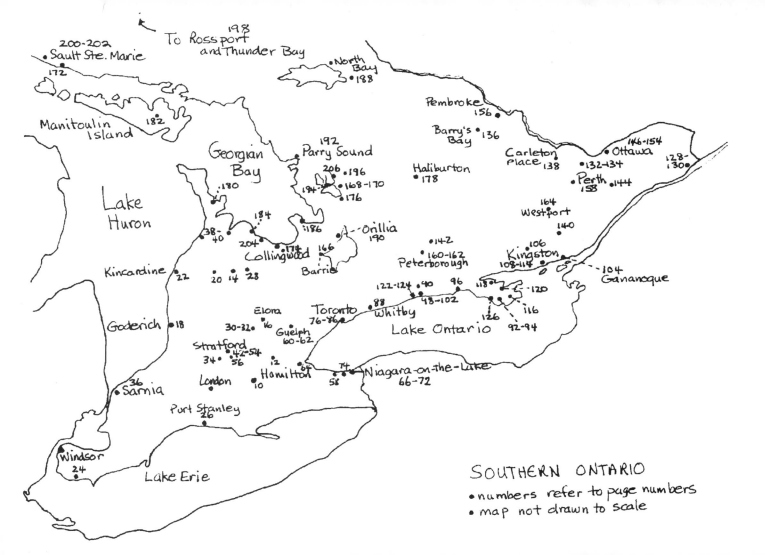

To Rossport
198
and Thunder Bay

200-202
Sault Ste. Marie
172

Manitoulin
Island
182

North
Bay
188

Lake
Huron

Georgian
Bay

Parry Sound
192
206 196
194 168-170
176

Haliburton
178

Pembroke
156

Barry's
Bay 136

Carleton
Place 138
132-134

Ottawa 146-154

128-130

Perth
158 144

180

184

186

Orillia
190

142

160-162
Peterborough

Westport
164
140

106
Kingston
108-114

104
Gananoque

38-40

204
174
Collingwood
166
Barrie

Kincardine
22
20 14 28

Goderich
18

Elora
16
Toronto
76-86
Guelph
60-62

122-124 40 96
88 48-102
Whitby

118
120

126 116
92-94

Lake Ontario

Stratford
34 42-54
56
12
Hamilton
64
58

74
Niagara-on-the-Lake
66-72

London
10

30-32

Sarnia
36

Port Stanley
26

Windsor
24

Lake Erie

SOUTHERN ONTARIO
• numbers refer to page numbers
• map not drawn to scale

On the Grand B&B

Don and Lisa Sylvester
119 Tutela Heights
R.R. 3
Brantford, ON N3T 5L6
519-752-2972

Best time to call: 9AM to 9PM
Season: all year
Rates: S $70-75, D $80-85
(includes GST) Enquire about off-season and longer stay discounts
Cards: VISA
Restrictions: smoking on outside covered patio only; no guests' pets
Facilities: 2 bedrooms (2 queen); 2 bathrooms (1 en suite with shower only; 1 private-use with combined shower/tub); living room for guests; central air
Parking: plenty on site
Breakfast: full
In residence: Purry and Jaumbie, the cats; young children, Blaire, Ben and Emma
Location: south Brantford near Alexander Graham Bell Homestead
Directions: from Hwy 403 take Davis Rd. S. (it becomes Brant Ave.) Follow signs over river for Bell Homestead. B&B is 400 metres past it.

In-the-know canoeists and business types have discovered On the Grand B&B – but you'll find it worth a visit even if you have no other reason to be in Brantford. For starters, you may want to sit awhile on the verandah – this 1907-built house is set high above the Grand River meandering through pastoral countryside. You may even be compelled to rent a canoe from the nearby Grand River Canoe Company.

Genial host Don Sylvester runs a home-based business, along with looking after the B&B and three young children, while wife Lisa goes out to work. And don't worry about the kids, besides staying away from the guest area, they're *very* well-behaved.

Decor throughout the house is comfortable, uncluttered and attractively coordinated. On the walls, besides a collection of limited edition prints, you'll find dried-flower swags draped over doors and windows. Upstairs, the three bedrooms are a good size and all have private bathrooms.

The White Room overlooks the river and has a queen-size bed. The bathroom's across the hall, so the Sylvesters provide bathrobes. The Bell Room also overlooks the river and has a queen-size bed, with a wicker chair and TV. From it you can see the Alexander Graham Bell homestead just down the road.

For breakfast the next morning you'll probably have Don's home-made bread and one of his specialties such as caramel-pear pancake with peameal bacon. After, if you like, take the path down to the Grand River and follow the trail along its banks – you'll soon be deep into spirit-soothing Carolinian forest.

10

- On the Grand B&B -

Here, a pastoral view of the often-elusive Grand River and, to soothe the spirit, a trek through Carolinian forest.

Kress Hill House

Nickolas and Donna Keglevich
127 Jacob St.
Cambridge, ON N3H 2T7
519-653-8728

Best time to call: anytime
Season: all year
Rates: S $55-75, D $75-95
Restrictions: children over 12 welcome; no smoking; no guests' pets
Facilities: 3 bedrooms (2 double, 1 queen); 3 bathrooms (1 en suite combined shower/tub, 1 shared with guests only with shower only, 1 downstairs 2-piece); drawing room for guests; central air
Parking: plenty on site
Breakfast: full
Location: an hour's drive either west of Toronto or east of London
Directions: from Hwy 401 take exit 278 (Hwy 8 East) towards Cambridge. Turn left onto Fountain Street; first left off Fountain is Jacob St

The approach to Kress Hill House is as if in a dream. White picket fence. Manicured grounds. And an 1845 ashlar limestone Gothic-style Victorian house astride the crest of a hill. Nick and Donna Keglevich are the maestros behind this home's transformation. True, it had superb bones – some of the most impressive millwork I've seen – but they've brought an elegance to the decor that's not easily surpassed by any B&B in this book. The drawing room's an indication. Botanical prints, black marble fireplace surround, mahogany furnishings and a green, rose and cream English-country decor.

Upstairs, the commodious Westover Room, has an en suite bathroom, and views over the sloping front lawn. Chippendale-style mahogany furnishings include a four-poster queen-size bed dressed in luxurious linens. The other two rooms share a bathroom down the hall. The Brunschwig has a double French provincial bed and among the attractive furnishings is a small collection of entomological and botanical prints. The Shumacher Room has a different look. Its double brass bed has a brown-and-taupe Chinoise-pattern bedcover. Military-style tables flank each side.

Nick and Donna are retired now, but they've spent most of their working lives together in the food and hospitality business. Evidence of their expertise is found at breakfast. A small but telling example: the fruit was clearly selected by someone with exacting standards. Donna had trekked all over town to search it out. The next course might be blueberry buttermilk pancakes, back bacon and cheddar quiche or whole wheat waffles with strawberry compote.

Kress Hill House

A house with superb bones – plus an extraordinary B&B.

Dr. James Gun Inn Bed & Breakfast

Shirley and Bill Iceton
283 Durham Rd. E.
Durham, ON N0G 1R0
519-369-6876 (tel/fax)
E-mail: gun.inn@bmts.com

Best time to call: anytime
Season: May 1 – Nov 30
Rates: S $55, D $60 (no taxes)
Restrictions: smoking outside, no guests' pets
Facilities: 3 bedrooms (1 twin-bedded, 1 double, 1 queen, extra double for overflow); 2 bathrooms shared by guests only (1 shower only, 1 shower/tub); 2nd floor common room for guests; telephone in guests' sitting room; fax and computer available
Parking: off-street for 6 cars
Breakfast: full
In residence: Alexandra, the cat (rarely seen by anyone)
Location: ½ hr S of Owen Sound; 1 hr N of Kitchener
Directions: N on Hwy 6 from lights in Durham to top of hill. Turn right on Durham Rd to second house on right (look for the 3-car coach house)

Thoroughbreds romp in the paddocks across the road from the Dr. James Gun Inn B&B and from its back gardens and patios your view is over scenic forest to the Saugeen river.

Hosts Shirley and Bill Iceton, like many, had wanted to move to a smaller community for their retirement. They'd spend their weekends driving from town to town looking for the right spot – and for the right house for B&B. The first time they saw this house they fell hard – but the price was too high. With patience and sheer luck, they finally nabbed it three years later when the price was too good to pass up.

When you first drive in, you notice the neoclassic doric columns of this home built in 1865 for the local doctor. Inside, the Icetons have laid cream wall-to-wall carpeting, but you'll be able to discern the original features of the house from the many architectural details they've restored.

Upstairs, is where you'll find the main guest area. Here, off the spacious room-sized hall you'll find three bedrooms, two bathrooms, and a cosy sitting room with TV, VCR and a selection of books and games. The attractive guest bedrooms all have monogrammed towels hung on Victorian blanket racks together with little niceties like soaps, shampoos and hand creams. You won't go wrong if you choose by bed size, queen, twin or double.

And if a special breakfast is one of the reasons you like staying at B&Bs, you'll be glad you booked here. The main course could be a bacon-and-vegetable cheese strata with pepper salsa and cherry tomatoes. Or how about mixed pancakes (banana, bacon, corn) with back bacon, maple syrup, apple sauce or sour cream.

By the way, there's a fourth bedroom the Icetons rent out if the whole place is taken over by a group. Increasingly, Shirley says, folks on self-planned bike tours are booking in. So why not gather some friends and off you go. Sounds like a plan ...

-Dr. James Gun Inn B&B-

Out-of-the-way Durham is well worth visiting for this B&B alone.

The Old Bissell House

Don and Jeanette Potter
84 Mill Street East
Elora, ON N0B 1S0
519-846-6695

Best time to call: 9 AM-10 PM
Season: all year
Rates: S $60-70, D $70-75 (no taxes)
Cards: VISA
Restrictions: not suitable for children, smoking on verandah, no guests' pets
Facilities: 4 bedrooms (1 double, 2 queen, 1 king which can be twins); 2 en suite bathrooms (1 with shower/tub, 1 2-piece), 1 bathroom shared by guests (shower/tub/Jacuzzi); living room with fireplace for guests, central air, telephone on main floor
Parking: off-street for 4 cars
Breakfast: full
Location: 30 mins from Kitchener; 1 hr 15 mins W of Toronto
Directions: from Hwy 401, take exit 295 (Hwy 6). Go north through Guelph to Fergus on Hwy 6. Elora is 5km W of Fergus on Cty Rd 18

My introduction to The Old Bissell House was through the back door. It was some entrance. A verandah runs across the back and the panelled door has sidelights and a transom window. Inside, the tiled foyer was beautifully decorated. Turns out it's only slightly less grand than the mirror-image front entrance. I was warmly welcomed by hosts, Don and Jeannette Potter, even though I'd phoned at the last minute, and they were busy decorating for a Christmas House Tour. (Of course, they had no idea who I was until the next morning, after I'd paid.)

I stayed in the misty green-and-rose Vadale Room with its en suite bathroom. Perfect. I was at the end of my research for this edition and feeling pooped. So I was quite contented to have a long soak in the tub, use some of the scented bath amenities and snuggle into the cannonball bed with an armload of magazines. It was the perfect room for a pamper. Like the others it has terry robes, clock radio, a window seat and small sitting area. The Carolyn Room has a two-piece bathroom en suite and shares the main bathroom with the other two rooms: the Grandview with iron-and-brass double bed and view of the river; and the Asha-Joy which has two single beds which can be made into king-size.

Next morning my breakfast was taken by candlelight in the dining room, part of the large attractive common area for guests. As a last-minute drop-in, at an awkward time, I had a simple omelette with the usual add-ons. For you, though, Jeannette will probably have something like mushroom-broccoli quiche or homemade Belgian waffles with fresh fruit and whipped cream.

You won't lack for things to do after breakfast. Elora is quite a tourist attraction, what with its gorge and quarry, restaurants, boutiques and artisans' studios. There's also opportunity to hike, walk, canoe, bike and fly fish. Even bounce along on a rubber tire in the Grand River if you fancy.

The Old Bissell House

Truly something special – and the back entrance is almost as grand as the front.

Twin Porches

Argie Strote
55 Nelson St. E.
Goderich, ON N7A 1R7
519-524-5505

Best time to call: before 11 PM
Season: May through October
Rates: S $40, D $50
(no taxes)
Restrictions: smoking outside
Facilities: 3 bedrooms; 2 queen, 1 double, 1 cot for child (ages 5-12) $10 extra; 1 bathroom shared only by guests (combined shower/tub); upstairs lounge, living room, porches and patio for guest use; air conditioning
Parking: on site, and legal on street overnight
Breakfast: full
Location: a 1 hour drive north of London, 3 hours west of Toronto, and 45 minutes from Stratford
Directions: 6 blocks north of the intersection of Hwys 8 and 21 in downtown Goderich (just across the road from Tourist Information)

Former Buttonville resident Argie Strote wanted to open a bed and breakfast place. She loved Victorian architecture, and Goderich was her favourite Ontario town. So she began a search for the perfect house. The way she did it is intriguing. She dropped letters into the mailboxes of all the homes she fancied, indicating her interest. One that particularly appealed had been in the same family since 1912. Argie waited. Two years later, Twin Porches was hers.

Try to arrive at Twin Porches after dark. The night lighting makes it look straight out of a romantic movie, set in the last century. If you do arrive in the day time though, you'll better appreciate the gardens surrounding the house. Either way, the effect is welcoming.

Inside, there's much to admire as well, including the three bedrooms upstairs. The Rose Room has a queen-size bed and is decorated in shades of rose; even the ceiling. The largest is the romantic-looking Blue Room with its woodwork and furni-ture painted white, including the four-poster double bed. The peach-and-cocoa Peach Room has a queen-size bed.

Breakfast has the usual range, and during it I had an animated chat with the gregarious host, all the while admiring the antiques. Argie's an inveterate collector. There was everything from a display of biscuit barrels to a group of paintings by William Henry Chandler, a landscape artist who worked at the turn of the century. Argie's overflow is on display in the front hall for guests who may want to buy. Before I left I bought an antique butter knife. A little something to add to my *own* collection.

— Twin Porches —

Try to arrive at Twin Porches after dark. The night lighting makes this house look straight out of a romantic movie, set at the turn of the century.

Victorian Manor

Ruth Peter-Nielsen and
Jannich Nielsen
500 9ᵗʰ Ave.
Hanover, ON N4N 2M3
519-364-1117 (tel/fax)

Best time to call: anytime
Languages: Danish
Season: all year
Rates: S $45, D $55 (no taxes)
Restrictions: smoking on verandah, no guests' pets
Facilities: 3 bedrooms (1 twin-bedded, 1 double, 1 single – plus another twin-bedded available if groups book); 1 bathroom shared with hosts (shower/tub); living room for guests; portable phone; fax available
Parking: off-street for 4-5 cars
Breakfast: full
In residence: Sparky and Pepper, the cats; Buffy, the Spaniel
Location: Hanover is on Hwy 4 mid-way between Durham and Walkerton; ¾ hr S of Owen Sound
Directions: In downtown Hanover watch for 9th Avenue north of Main St

The warm feelings I have for Victorian Manor can be explained by any number of things. First off, I phoned to book at 6:30 on a Sunday night in October. Hosts Ruth Peter-Nielsen and Jannich Nielsen were just heading off to church, but they said I was welcome, they'd leave a key with a neighbour. When I drove up, the outside lighting brought out the home's architectural features. Inside, I was greeted by soft classical music, and as I looked around I was captivated by the ornate Victorian woodwork, the light glancing off leaded glass and the patina of wide pine-board floors. It felt warm, cosy and inviting even with no-one there to greet me. That takes some doing.

Jannich showed up earlier than Ruth, who had family commitments. A caring, gracious man, who retains much of his native Danish accent, he gave me Melaleuca tea, a herbal blend for those who have trouble sleeping (me), along with some baking that Ruth had made for their tea room (open for groups by reservation).

Upstairs, as I climbed into bed, the subtle scent of lavender wafted from the sheets, a further inducement to good sleep. I stayed in the Queen Victoria Room with an antique double bed. Another is The Prince Albert which has a single, and another, The Study, has two singles. As for bathrooms, there *is* only "one" and it *is* shared with the hosts. In effect, though, it's two rooms; one for the toilet and another large room for the tub and sink.

The next morning, Ruth prepared the best omelette I've ever tasted. It was topped with a dollop of yogurt and accompanied by homemade chutney and served on a plate decorated with pansies. After breakfast I was off to do more research for this book, but if you stay, there are several golf courses nearby, plus cross-country ski trails and nature walks which follow the winding Saugeen River.

Victorian Manor

*A warm and welcoming home
with a Victorian ambiance.*

Hanks' Heritage House

Tom and Margot Hanks
776 Princes St.
Kincardine, ON N2Z 1Z5
519-396-7991

Best time to call: before 9 AM or after 5 PM
Season: all year
Rates: S $40-50, D $50-60 (no taxes)
Restrictions: enquire about guests' pets
Facilities: 3 bedrooms (2 double, 1 twin-bedded); 1 bathroom shared only by guests, 1 private bathroom (combined shower/tub); several common areas
Parking: available
Breakfast: full
In residence: an assortment of bulldogs, real and otherwise
Location: a 35-minute drive north of Goderich and an hour-and-a-half northwest of Kitchener-Waterloo
Directions: from Queen St (the main street) turn east on Durham Market Square. Turn left onto Princes St

Hanks' Heritage House, built in 1870, is one of the most impressive homes in this summer resort town. Formerly owned, at one time or another, by three of the town's leading businessmen, this 13-room Victorian house is now home to the Hanks; Tom works for Ontario Hydro, and Margot is a real estate broker. You can spot the house by the distinctive widow's walk and large sun room on its south side.

There are lots of places to gather for fun or quiet times – the den with books and TV; the formal rose-and-blue parlour with grand piano; the sun room, with its original clay tile floor, filled with wicker and plants; or the large in-ground pool in the backyard. There's even a pinball machine and a pool table.

The bedrooms are on the second floor, and decorated in shades of brown, with pink, gold or blue accents. The one with private bath has twin beds and antique furniture. The others contain a blend of antiques and reproduction furniture. My favourite was the beige-and-blue room on the second floor, which has its own sun room (more plants and wicker) and an antique doll design in the wallpaper.

After a full breakfast in the dining room, you may want to walk it off. A good start is a stroll around the grounds since the Hanks are keen gardeners. If you're a rose fancier, and time your visit right, you'll find lots to ooh and aah about.

-Hanks' Heritage House-

It doesn't take much to spot this 13-room Victorian home. It has a distinctive widow's walk and huge sun roon on its south side. Inside, most of the house is given over to B&B guests.

The Wedding House Bed & Breakfast

Linda and Tom Gelinas
98 Main St. E.
Kingsville, ON N9Y 1A4
519-733-3928
E-mail: wedding@mnsi.net

Best time to call: anytime
Season: all year
Rates: S $55-70, D $60-75 (no taxes)
Cards: VISA/MC
Restrictions: well-behaved children welcome, no smoking, no guests' pets
Facilities: 4 bedrooms (2 kings, can be twins, 1 double, 1 queen); 3 bathrooms (1 en suite with shower, 1 main floor shower only, 1 second floor shower/tub); central air, parlour for guests; phone available
Parking: off-street for 5 cars
Breakfast: full
In residence: Pepper, the Collie
Location: 30 mins S of Windsor and U.S. border; 30 mins from Hwy 401
Directions: from Hwy 401, exit at Hwy 77 to Leamington. S on 77 through Leamington, turn right on Seacliff Dr (Cty Rd. 20). Drive 12 km to Kingsville to 2nd house on right before 2nd lights

The lengths I go to to research this book! (And the shenanigans my travel companions have to put up with.) I was determined to stay at The Wedding House since I knew it was the area's best candidate for this book. Trouble was they were full. And my friend and I needed two beds. Well, there *was* one small room that could be set up with a second bed (making for wall-to-wall bed) if I insisted. I insisted. Hosts Linda and Tom Gelinas kept their friendly demeanour throughout, even though they must have wondered what was up.

The first thing anyone wants to know about this B&B is where the name, "The Wedding House", comes from. Turns out that the house was a wedding gift to the original owners from the bride's parents. Later, all the newly-married couples in town were photographed out front because of the attractive verandah. Nowadays, brides book the whole house for wedding parties; but in between times this is a fine place for *you* to stay.

The four guest bedrooms are upstairs. Three rooms share two bathrooms; one up and one down-stairs. Right now, the Wedding Room is the most popular with its bay window, king-size (or twin) bed and comfortable seating area. But I have no doubt The Library is destined to be the most popular room; done in dark greens and burgundies, it features a new *en suite* bathroom. Another king-size bed is found in the pretty Rose Room. As for my friend and I, we squeezed into Calee's Room – fine for one or two people if you don't insist on an extra bed!

Next morning, for breakfast, we had blueberry pancakes but yours could be French toast or bacon, scrambled eggs and hash browns. After, your days will be full with visits to Point Pelee National Park, Colasanti's Tropical Gardens, the Jack Miner Bird Sanctuary and several historical sites, all less than 20 minutes away.

- the Wedding House Bed & Breakfast -

*Make The Wedding House B&B
your base, and take in all this
interesting area has on offer.*

Mitchell House

Marlene and Jerry Robinson
493 George St.
P.O. Box 725
Port Stanley, ON N0L 2A0
519-782-4707

Best time to call: evenings
Season: all year
Rates: S $40, D $50 (no taxes)
Restrictions: children welcome, no smoking inside, enquire about guests' pets
Facilities: 4 bedrooms (4 double beds, 1 room also has a single); 2 bathrooms shared with guests (1 private with tub & shower, 1 shared with other guests shower only); large common area and porch for guests
Parking: in circular drive
Breakfast: full
In residence: Holmes, the sleuth cat
Location: a 2-hour drive, either west of Toronto or east of Windsor
Directions: from Hwy 401 take Hwy 4 south to Port Stanley. Turn right at only light, go over bridge, and follow road about 1 km

With its fishing village atmosphere and wide stretch of Lake Erie beach, picturesque Port Stanley has been drawing summer crowds for years. In the 1940s the Stork Club attracted 6,500 people a night to its dance floor. *It* burned down in 1979 but there's still ample reason to visit – golf, shopping, summer theatre and good restaurants are all close by.

Set apart from the busy beach action is the quiet farmhouse-style B&B run by Marlene and Jerry Robinson. You take a dead-end road leading out of town and a minute later pull into the circular drive flanked by a rustic cedar-rail fence. Along its length, depending on the month, you'll find roses, orange lilies, or black-eyed Susans.

You reach the four guest bedrooms, all on the second floor, by climbing a spiral staircase in the guest lounge. The rooms are light, with lots of white and pastels in the decorating. The largest guest bedroom has two beds and a private en suite bathroom. Two other rooms have pine plank floors and shutters, while another has a white iron bed covered with a quilt in a pink-and-blue log cabin design. These three share a bathroom which has two entrances, one of which opens directly into one of the bedrooms. Just remember to unlock both doors when you leave.

You're welcome, of course, to use the guest lounge or you can join Marlene and Jerry in the less-formal family room, with its floor-to-ceiling stone fireplace and country decor.

Breakfast in cooler weather may be bacon and eggs with hash browns, served up on the pine harvest table. Or, in warmer weather, you're more likely to get Marlene's version of banana French toast with fruit sauce, taken outside on the back patio.

- Mitchell House -

The fishing village atmosphere and sandy beach aren't the only reasons to stop awhile in Port Stanley.

Glen Elg Country Inn Bed & Breakfast

Jennifer and Steve Cambria
R.R. 1
Priceville, ON N0C 1K0
519-369-2858

Best time to call: anytime
Season: all year
Rates: S or D $65 (taxes incl.)
Cards: VISA
Restrictions: children over 12 welcome, smoking outside on porch, no guests' pets
Facilities: 3 bedrooms (1 twin-bedded, 2 queen); 3 en suite bathrooms; common area adjacent to dining area for guests; telephone in kitchen
Parking: off-street
Breakfast: full
In residence: Brandy, Golden Lab and Akita mix; Taffy, Pekinese and Pomeranian mix
Location: on 40 acres near the gateway to the Beaver Valley, 10 mins to town of Flesherton
Directions: 1 hr 45 min N of Toronto between Durham and Flesherton (Hwy 4). 1 km S on Grey Road 23

Frazzled city folk, take heed. Stratford-trained chef, Jennifer Cambria and husband, Steve, bought this old Ontario farmhouse; restored, renovated and decorated; put in en suite bathrooms and created a relaxing country house getaway. Even if it's out of your way, you'll be amply rewarded if you plan to spend a little time here. And if you arrive by Grey Coach Bus in nearby Flesherton, the Cambrias will arrange to pick you up and drop you off.

Upon entering, you'll see the smallish common area to your right and you'll discover it's easy to sink into the down-filled sofa and feel your cares float away. Upstairs, is where you'll find two of the guest bedrooms. The medium-size Twin Room has twin beds with antique headboards. There's a sitting area with wing back chair and reading lamp. The Green Queen Room's bed is covered with a down comforter in winter and handcrafted quilt in summer. Its wing chair is a recliner. A third room is accessed by way of the narrow back stairs, off the kitchen. Called the Kitchen Queen, it's my favourite. A large room with cathedral ceiling and three windows facing west and north, it's furnished in Canadiana antique reproductions.

Come with a group of friends and arrange for one of Jennifer's cooking lessons – or just let her come up with something delectable for dinner. The average price for dinner is usually somewhere between $20 and $30 (taxes included). A special five-course meal on, say, New Years Eve costs more. BYOB.

After a restful night's sleep, you'll come down to a breakfast that starts with a juice mixed with sparkling wine. Jennifer always has yogurt, granola and fruit available, plus something baked like croissants or muffins. The main dish varies, perhaps eggs Benedict with smoked salmon or French toast infused with cranberry. After, you can roam around the Cambria's forty acres or set out to explore the countryside. In winter, the Beaver Valley ski hills are just half an hour away.

28

- Glen Elg Country Inn B&B -

The romance of a country house and the downright good cooking of a Stratford-trained chef.

The Old Flax Mill Guest House

Anne and Barry Noice
50 Glasgow St. North
Conestogo, ON N0B 1N0
519-664-3600
E-mail: BENoice@aol.com

Best time to call: 9AM to 9PM
Season: all year
Rates: S $60, D $70
Restrictions: not suitable for children; smoking outside only; no guests' pets
Facilities: 2 bedrooms (2 queen); 2 bathrooms shared by guests only (1 combined shower/tub, 1 downstairs with shower only); living room, verandah, porch and patio shared by guests; central air
Parking: plenty on site
Breakfast: full
In residence: Zoë, the friendly Labrador Retriever
Location: 10-minute drive north of Kitchener-Waterloo, 5 minutes east of St. Jacobs
Directions: from Hwy 401 take Hwy 8 west (exit 278) into Kitchener. Take Hwy 86 north to Cty Rd 17. Turn right. Go 3 kms to Conestogo. Go left on Glasgow

The Mennonite tourist town of St. Jacobs is exceptionally busy in high summer, and busy enough at other times of the year, so it's nice to know about The Old Flax Mill Guest House, just five minutes east of St Jacobs in Conestogo. Here in this quiet village, on a quiet side street, you'll find Anne and Barry Noice's recently built colonial-style home – a retirement retreat for themselves and for you, a retreat-like getaway.

Named for the nineteenth-century mill across the road, this B&B is set in a clearing, with woods around, and lawns sloping down to the waterway that once powered the mill. Streamside, you'll find a large stone patio with summer furniture – a relaxing place to unwind to the soothing sounds of a nearby waterfall. With spirits revived, you're welcome to play croquet, badminton or bocce ball. Even billiards. There's a pool table in the old livery stable at the entrance to the property.

Inside the home, the large wainscotted living room has an extensive library and music centre with organ. Upstairs, everything matches in the broadloomed guest bedrooms, which feature considerate touches like bathrobes, clock radios, reading lights and Body Shop toiletries. Both rooms have queen-size beds and a couple of cane chairs.

Retired high school teachers, Anne and Barry, have lots of interests. Barry, especially, likes to bake. If his Indian sweet pumpkin bread from New Mexico's not on the morning's menu, he'll whip up something else like Mennonite carrot bread or cheddar-cheese muffins. To be followed by a main dish, perhaps banana souffle or an omelet flavoured with fresh herbs from Anne's garden. All accompanied by candlelight and soft music.

- The Old Flax Mill Guest House -

A retreat-like hideaway in a tranquil setting.

Schweitzer Haus Bed & Breakfast

Shirley and Paul Schweitzer
RR 3, Wallenstein, ON N0B 2S0
519-699-4439 (fax 699-5074)
E-mail: schweitzer@golden.net

Best time to call: 10 AM to 10 PM
Season: all year
Rates: S $55, D $65 (no taxes)
Restrictions: enquire about
children, no smoking, no guests'
pets
Facilities: 2 bedrooms (1 twin-
bedded, 1 queen); 1 bathroom
shared by guests (shower only);
common area adjacent to
bedrooms for guests; telephone is
available
Parking: off-street for many cars
Breakfast: generous continental
Location: 5 mins W of St. Jacobs
near Kitchener-Waterloo
Directions: from Hwy 401, exit
Hwy 8 W, then take Hwy 86 N to
Regional Rd 17 (stop light). Turn
left (W) and drive 7.6 km to
Schweitzer Haus on right side

With St. Jacobs such a popular tourist destination it's wise to have a *couple* of good B&Bs up your sleeve. So here's another. Just five minutes west of town, you'll find a Quebecois-style log house built in 1987 by Shirley and Paul Schweitzer. Upon arrival your amiable hosts will show you the B&B area on the lower level. You'll find the shared bathroom, two guest bedrooms and a country-furnished common area with large picture window overlooking the nearby bird-feeders and meadows beyond.

The Lady Sara Room has twin beds done in peach and sage green with nice touches like Limoges china knobs on the pine doors. The crisp sheets are line-dried (weather permitting) and ironed. The Log Cabin Room's name is inspired by the design of its queen-size bed's quilt. Both rooms have individual thermostats. The large shared bathroom serves double duty – travellers who've been on the road awhile will appreciate the laundry facilities there.

Now, if you're a privacy die-hard there's a convenient side entrance on the B&B level. If not, you'll enjoy mingling with Shirley and Paul in their large open-concept great room with sixteen-foot stone fire-place. When I commented on the quality of the stonework, I learned it was built by a Spanish stonemason who said his descend-ents had been stonemasons for *1200* years! Though large, the room has a cosy, inviting feel and it's here you'll be offered tea, cookies and lively conversation in the evening.

Next morning, the Schweitzers provide the kind of continental breakfast I like. Juice, fresh fruit, cereal, cheeses, bread and homemade preserves always available. Plus something like Paul's Chelsea buns. Or Shirley's delicious baked apples with oatmeal scones. Recently, they made the apple dish for some Japanese visitors with a camera crew in tow, and the resulting video is now being shown around Japan to entice visitors to the area. Should work.

– Schweitzer Haus B&B –

Hospitable hosts in a country-side B&B just five minutes outside St. Jacobs

Eagleview Manor

Bob and Pat Young
Box 3183, 178 Widder St. East
St. Marys, ON N4X 1A8
519-284-1811

Best time to call: anytime
Season: all year
Rates: S $50-65, D $60-70 (no taxes)
Restrictions: no smoking in house, no guests' pets
Facilities: 3 bedrooms (1 queen, 1 double, 1 double plus single); 3 bathrooms (1 Jacuzzi, 1 shower only, 1 with shower downstairs); living room and verandah for guests; in ground pool
Parking: legal overnight on street
Breakfast: full
Location: St. Marys is 15-minute drive from Stratford and 30 minutes from London
Directions: at east end of downtown St. Marys turn N on Church St. Go 2 blocks to Widder St. Turn right. B&B is first house

St. Marys is a good base for Stratford theatre-goers. And, situated on a tree-lined street of magnificent old homes, Eagleview Manor is a fine place to stay. Upon walking in, you're struck by the entrance hall's sweeping staircase. To the right, guests have use of the large living room, and upstairs, three lovely bedrooms. The queen-bedded Fireside Room has a working fireplace plus sitting area with wing chairs in its bay window. The Rose Room's double bed has a lace canopy and its single bed is made up with bolsters and pillows to resemble a couch. As well, there's the popular Eagleview Room which has a furnished eight-by-twenty-foot balcony overlooking the town. Out in the hall you'll find a table with cookies and everything you need for tea, coffee or hot chocolate.

Next morning, Pat offers breakfast in the formal oak dining room highlighted by several stained glass windows. She does all the usual breakfast dishes and sometimes branches out to do peach pancakes, blueberry strata or Belgian waffles. And something else. If you're there with a group, and have reserved *in advance,* she'll do thoroughly-decadent afternoon teas with little sandwiches and baked specialties – it's $10 per person for an elaborate Victorian Tea with all the trimmings. A great way to take a winter break with a group of good friends. To work up an appetite ahead of time (and justify the calories) you could go cross-country skiing on the nearby Wildwood trails or even ski right from Eagleview's back door along Trout Creek.

There's also much to enjoy in the town itself, especially if you're interested in architecture. Many of the buildings are made of stone, including one on the main street that was built as an opera house. Most of the stone came out of a quarry which is now the largest outdoor pool in Canada. And another attraction is scheduled to open soon – the Canadian Baseball Hall of Fame – Pat can keep you up to bat – whoops, up to date.

- Eagleview Manor -

High on a hill overlooking the town, this B&B offers a fine alternative for the Stratford theatre-goer and an indulgent winter-break for others.

Doon's Beach Bed & Breakfast

Bob and Audrey Hamilton
3889 Ferne Ave.
Box 18, Bonnie Doon
R.R. 2
Camlachie, ON N0N 1E0
519-899-2962

Best time to call: anytime
Season: all year
Rates: June 15 to Sep 15: S $65,
D $75 (other times it's $55/65)
Restrictions: no children; no
smoking; no guests' pets
Facilities: 1 guest suite; queen-
size in bedroom, love seat pull-
out in sitting room; en suite
bathroom with shower only;
sitting room with eating area and
small kitchen
Parking: on site
Breakfast: full
Location: 25 kms northeast of
Sarnia; 3 kms north of Camlachie
Directions: from Hwy 402, take
exit Hwy 21 north. Drive to
County Rd. 11 (Aberarder Line).
Turn left and go to County Rd 7
(Lake Shore Rd). Cross over and
take immediate right onto
Bonnie Doon Rd. Proceed ½ km
to hillside home on corner

There's only one suite at Doon's Beach B&B, but it's a beauty. Bob and Audrey Hamilton built this Cape Cod-style home in 1990 on the side of a hill in the quiet beach community of Bonnie Doon on Lake Huron, just north of Sarnia. The guest suite, with its own entrance, is on the lower level.

Bob still works in the oil business, while ex-travel agent Audrey looks after the B&B. Widely travelled themselves, they've thought of everything. Not only do you have fresh, attractively furnished quarters, but there's a TV, books, CD and tape player (with an extensive library of CDs and tapes), *and* a fully-equipped kitchen with a microwave. *Plus* there's a gas fireplace and outside barbecue. As for breakfast, Audrey brings it to your suite and complies with dietary requests.

This is a place for memories. The walls hold photos of the Hamilton's travel memories. And, borrowing an idea from Leacock award winner Bill Richardson's book, "The Bachelor Brothers B&B", Audrey provides a B&B Cottage Journal where guests are encouraged to write an interesting anecdote about themselves. Most happily comply and you'll find tales for all to share.

There's also the meditative ambiance of the surrounding gardens which have been designed to attract butterflies. Or you can take this contemplative mood to the wide, secluded beach and walk for miles.

- Doon's Beach B&B -

Memories are made of this.

Crescent Manor

Isabel and Harold Timmins
48 Albert St. N.
P.O. Box 62
Southampton, ON N0H 2L0
519-797-5637

Best time to call: anytime
Season: May through Oct
(enquire about other times)
Rates: S $35, D $45 (no taxes)
Restrictions: no smoking, no
guests' pets
Facilities: 3 bedrooms; (2 double,
1 twin-bedded); 2 bathrooms
shared only by guests (1 combined
shower/tub, 1 2-piece); common
room, lounge and screened-in
porch for guests
Parking: off street
Breakfast: continental plus
Location: Southampton is on
Lake Huron just south of the
Bruce Peninsula. It's a 25-minute
drive southwest of Owen Sound
Directions: Crescent Manor is on
Hwy 21 (Albert St in town)
across from the Presbyterian
Church

This yellow brick Victorian house takes its name from the shape of the large lawn out front. Built in 1890, it has many lovely architectural details, including the original hardwood and pine floors, a handsome bannister, and beautiful wood mouldings and fretwork. I was welcomed into the foyer by Harold, recently retired from keeping Ontario Hydro's nuclear generating machines in good working order. He and Isabel like skiing, auction sales and bridge. So if you're a bridge player there's a chance you could get to play a hand.

The three bedrooms upstairs are comfortably furnished with a mix of antiques and "early matrimonial" as Isabel calls it. The Gold Room has Andrew Malcolm twin beds, an antique desk and a comfortable chair with reading lamps. The Garden Room contains a double brass bed with a view of – you guessed it – the garden. It's decorated in white eyelet and is a favourite with many guests. The Green Room, at the back of the house near the bathroom, is often chosen by older people. You'll find some thoughtful touches in the rooms: candies, fruit or flowers. And a needle and thread for emergency mends.

Breakfast is continental plus and sometimes you'll be treated to homemade scones or coffee cake instead of the usual muffins. After, you can get to know Southampton. It's a great town for a bicycle – easy to get around, with beautiful old homes. And, just a short drive away, you'll find a museum and amphitheatre with a nature trail. But the best part is the beach – Lake Huron has some of the most beautiful in Ontario. Southampton's is only three minutes from Crescent Manor by car.

- Crescent Manor -

Southampton's a great town for a bicycle – easy to get around, with a beach and beautiful old homes. Crescent Manor's one of them.

39

Solomon Knechtel House

John and Marty Church
106 Victoria St. S.
Southampton, ON N0H 2L0
519-797-2585
E-mail: j.church@bmts.com

Best time to call: anytime
Season: all year
Rates: S or D $55-85 (no taxes)
Restrictions: smoking outside, no guests' pets
Facilities: 3 bedrooms (1 queen, 2 double); 2 bathrooms (1 en suite, 1 shared, both with shower/tub); main floor living room for guests; telephone in 2 bedrooms
Parking: off-street for 4-5 cars
Breakfast: full
Location: Southampton is on Lake Huron, 2 hrs N of Kitchener and 3 hrs NW of Toronto
Directions: 1 block N of Hwy 21 at corner of Morpeth and Victoria Sts

Nothing but the best for the original owner of this exceptional home. After all, builder Solomon Knechtel owned a prominent wood-turning factory in town, so it was important his home be a showpiece. Sadly, though, a hundred or so years later it had lapsed into disrepair. Along came some renovators who saw its potential and, following Solomon's lead, they restored the house to its original grandeur. Then, after putting so much into it, rather than sell to just anyone, they sold to their mother Marty and her husband John Church. And so once again, it's a showpiece – this time for B&B guests to exclaim over.

Upon entering, you'll see immediately what I mean – there's an outstanding staircase with elaborate turned spindles leading up to the second floor. Here is where you'll find the three guest bedrooms. The largest is painted sea-green with stencilled trim and has a shuttered bay window. There's an antique queen-size bed with two wing chairs. Its huge en suite

bathroom has a stencilled wood floor with a shower stall and claw foot tub. The other two guest bedrooms share a bathroom. One is dark green with an antique double bed and contains a wicker chair with ottoman for reading. The other is a soft peach-and-ivory stripe with an iron-and-brass double bed and wicker chair.

Next morning, you'll find yourself in an elaborate Tuscan-red dining room with chandelier, ceiling medallion and crown mouldings all competing for your eye. Even though Marty works (she's a nurse in a doctor's office) she usually prepares a full breakfast with a main dish like a cheese omelette, French toast or Belgian waffles with fresh strawberries in season.

After, Marty or John can direct you to fishing excursions, bicycle trails, golf courses, good tennis courts, or the sandy beach just three blocks away. John's a professional sign-maker and his shop's out back so if Marty's off to work, he's around to help you out.

– Soloman Knechtel House –

They just don't make them like this anymore – a truly exceptional home.

41

Angel's In Bed & Breakfast

Chuck and Anita Summers
208 Church St.
Stratford, ON N5A 2R6
519-271-9651

Best time to call: afternoon or evening
Season: all year
Rates: S or D $75-85 (no taxes)
Restrictions: no children, no smoking, no guests' pets
Facilities: 3 bedrooms (1 double, 1 queen, 1 king, can be twins); 3 en suite bathrooms (all shower only); parlour and gazebo porch for guests; telephone in dining room
Parking: off-street for 3 cars
Breakfast: full
In residence: teens, Erin and Tara; pre-teen, Bronwen; Fluffy, the rabbit, kept out of guest quarters
Location: Stratford is 2 hrs W of Toronto and 3 hrs NW of Detroit
Directions: from Toronto, turn left from Ontario onto Church St; from London or Detroit, turn left from Erie St onto Cambria. Go to Church

Throughout Angel's In B&B you'll find evidence of host Anita Summers' remarkable hand-stencilling. It has a very nineties look: soft, subtle, and not a hint of "country". Husband, Chuck was a big help too. Together they stencilled the guest parlour walls in an old-rose damask which you'll see upon passing through the parlour's eight-foot double doors. Here, antiques mingle eclectically with a vintage sofa and chairs around the Victorian-tiled wood-burning fireplace. A magnificent old English billiard table occupies the other half of the room where there's an entire wall of Cries of London lithographs.

You'll find more stencilling upstairs. In the Fireplace Room, it's on the walls – a gold damask pattern enhances the room's English-manor look with its curtained queen-sized four-poster bed. The fireplace works, too. Walls of the Garden Room are also stencilled, this time with a casual arrangement of birds and flowers. The twin beds can be put together as a king, and the colours of the room are captured in the pastel-plaid taffeta dust ruffles and window blinds. A much-admired feature of the bathroom (they're all en suite here) is the floor strewn with stencilled flowers and berries. There's a French country house feel in the Continental Room where Anita's used a buff-and-raspberry toile de Jouy fabric for the curtains and dust ruffle on the iron-and-brass double bed. A slipper chair is covered in a multicoloured French damask. The Summers painted wide buff-and-cream stripes on the walls, and Anita's done the floor in a medieval fleur-de-lis design.

As for breakfast, it's at 9 each morning and Anita changes the menu daily so if you're there for a few days, each one's an adventure. She shines with dishes like creme-brulee grapefruit, yogurt-currant scones, caramel-peach French toast, and buttermilk-berry-crumble coffee cake.

— Angel's In Bed & Breakfast —

The value is heavenly at Angel's In B&B.

Avonview Manor

Gail and Lynne Doupé
63 Avon St.
Stratford, ON N5A 5N5
519-273-4603
E-mail: avonview@cyg.net

Best time to call: anytime
Season: all year
Rates: S or D $70-80, Triple $105, Quad $130 (PST included)
Restrictions: no smoking, no guests' pets
Facilities: 4 bedrooms (3 queen, 1 with 4 single beds); 3 bathrooms shared by guests (1 shower/tub on main floor, 1 split bathroom on 2nd floor with shower/tub, 2 private with shower only); living room/solarium shared by guests; guest kitchen on 2nd floor; in-ground pool and hot tub
Parking: for 6 cars in drive
Breakfast: full
In residence: Katy, the golden retriever and Scud the Shih Tzu
Location: see first Stratford entry
Directions: follow Ontario St (main street) onto Huron. Go across river to first stoplight. Turn left on John. Go 3 blocks to Avon St. Turn left

Avonview Manor is aptly-named. Its large back lawn edges on parkland which follows the Avon River on its course through town. It certainly appealed to Gail and Lynne Doupé, sisters who left jobs in Kingston and Toronto to start their B&B a few years ago. The entrance foyer of their attractive Edwardian home is decorated with quarter-cut oak panels and a mural which was painted at the end of the first world war.

You get the best view of the river from the large sun room – it has 12 windows. This room is perfect for families because it has its own bathroom, four single beds and a separate sitting room.

The queen-bedded Green Room has leaded and stained glass windows and an antique wicker rocker. The Rose Room has a forest-green loveseat and its queen-size four poster bed is covered with a Mennonite quilt. These two rooms share two bathrooms. On the second floor, where the bedrooms are, the water closet is separate from the room containing tub and sink. Downstairs, there's another full bathroom, so line-ups should be non existent.

More beautiful windows in the Blue Room with its floral quilt, queen-size bed and natural wicker furniture. Its en suite bathroom has a shower only.

There are some other things you'll appreciate as well. Such as a pitcher of ice water after a long, hot drive. Or free use of the in ground pool and hot tub.

— Avonview Manor —

For the best view of the river book the room with the 12 windows. It has four beds and a sun porch – perfect for families.

Blackwater House

Judith Horner and
Hammond Bentall
122 Douglas St
Stratford, ON N5A 5P6
519-273-6490 (fax 273-2544)

Best time to call: anytime
Languages: French, German
Season: May - Oct
Rates: S $100, D $125 (no taxes)
Restrictions: children over 16 welcome, smoking on porch, no guests' pets
Facilities: 3 bedrooms (1 double incl. adjoining room with single bed, 1 queen plus single, 1 king); 3 en suite bathrooms (1 whirlpool tub with hand shower, 2 shower only); drawing room for guests; telephone available
Parking: off-street for 4 cars
Breakfast: full
In residence: Jackson & Briggs, the Jack Russell terriers; Fortnum & Mason, the cats
Location: central Stratford
Directions: head west on Ontario St and follow it over river onto Huron St. Douglas St is first left turn opposite the gas station

Good value figures prominently in my decision about which B&Bs to invite into this book. Now, Stratford has any number of B&Bs with rooms circa $125 double. Pick any one and, no doubt, you'll have a fine place to stay. But I wanted to offer readers my opinion of the *best in the price category –* my pick is the tasteful Blackwater House.

Located on a quiet residential street, you're a mere 10-minute walk from downtown and the Avon and Tom Patterson theatres. Or a 20-minute walk from the Festival Theatre. Inside, hosts Judith Horner and Hammond Bentall have done extensive renovations of this 1880s Victorian home. The style throughout is very much English-country-house with imported British silver, pictures and antique furniture – not surprising since both are English-born. Outside, there's an in ground pool surrounded by patios and manicured gardens. Guests are welcome to take a dip, swim a few laps or enjoy lively conversation in the sunshine.

Inside, there's a pleasant guest drawing room with gas fireplace and whimsical watercolours painted by the talented Judith. Upstairs, all three guest bedrooms are beautifully decorated and have en suite bathrooms. The Master Bedroom has a king-size bed, and its bathroom a whirlpool tub with hand shower. Another room has a queen-size bed plus a single. The third is actually a suite of two rooms; one with a double bed and the other with a single.

Next morning, the breakfast side dishes are laid out on the antique carpenter's workbench in the dining room. Always juice, muesli, yogurt, croissants and other breads. Plus Hammond's artfully-arranged plate of five or so fresh fruits. Then, befitting the hosts' heritage, you may well be served English-style scrambled eggs with tomato and bacon. After, have your second cup of coffee out on the back porch overlooking the gardens and take your time deciding about your day.

- Blackwater House -

An intelligent renovation, especially for B&B, in the traditional English style.

Chez Nous at Granny's Cottage

Rosaire Roy and Faye Schaus-Roy
111 Queen St.
Stratford, ON N5A 4N2
519-273-3493

Best time to call: anytime
Languages: French
Season: all year
Rates: S or D $75 (no taxes)
Restrictions: no children, smoking outdoors, no guests' pets
Facilities: 1 bedroom (1 queen); 1 bathroom shared with hosts (shower/tub); living room, dining room shared with hosts; mobile phone, fax available if necessary
Parking: off-street for 1 car
Breakfast: full
Location: 1½ hrs from Toronto; 1 hr E of Lake Huron
Directions: central Stratford about 1 block from Festival Theatre. Enter Stratford via Hwy 7/8 that becomes Ontario St. Turn N on Queen St to 111

Readers of previous editions of this book may recall my story of being sick and stormstayed at a B&B called Chez Nous. And how hosts Rosaire Roy and Faye Schaus-Roy, took such good care of me, that I felt much better when I left next morning, the storm's snowy rage finally spent. Sadly, Chez Nous is no more. But fret not, Faye and Rosaire have moved just around the corner.

Here's what happened. Everyone in the neighbourhood knew Granny Ratz. And Faye and Rosaire were no exception – they fell in love with her and visited often. *And* they loved her 1940s cottage-style house. They even hoped that some day it would be theirs. Sadly Granny died, having lived into her nineties, and the house went on the market. With fate on their side, the Roys sold Chez Nous and bought the cottage. Faye is convinced Granny was rooting for them all the way. Hence the name of this special B&B.

The Roys have undertaken extensive renovations to update and redecorate the home. There's only one guest bedroom here, the Kamouraska, and it's a lovely one. Its walls are buttery yellow accented by a large leaded-glass window and lovely linens dress its queen-size sleigh bed. As before, you share the bathroom with the hosts, but since they have another they use when guests are around, it's not *really* sharing. In any event, it's exceptionally clean and neat, and none of their personal belongings intrude.

Breakfast varies – it could be an omelette, souffle or some new recipe Faye's found appealing. And, of course, fruit, croissants and other add-ons.

And, oh yes, as at their previous B&B, you'll be within hearing range of the Festival Theatre's bugles trumpeting the start of the play. Time to skedaddle. Two minutes will get you there, just in time for the dimming of the house lights.

-Chez Nous at Granny's Cottage-

You'll feel like you're visiting good friends who just happen to live a block from the Festival Theatre. Lucky you.

Deacon House

Dianna Hrysko and Mary Allen
101 Brunswick St.
Stratford, ON N5A 3L9
519-273-2052

Best time to call: anytime
Season: all year
Rates: S $85-105, D $95-115
(plus PST & GST). Off-season
rates
Cards: VISA
Restrictions: enquire about
children, no smoking, no guests'
pets
Facilities: 6 bedrooms; (1 with
twin beds, 3 with doubles, 2 with
queen); 6 bathrooms (5 en suite,
1 private-use; all have combined
shower/tub); living room, 2nd-
floor sitting room for guests; air
conditioners in bedrooms
Parking: small lot at side
Breakfast: continental plus
In residence: cats, Emerald and
Offence, kept out of guest area
Location: see first Stratford entry
Directions: from Ontario St. (the
main street) at east end of
downtown, turn south on Nile St.
Go 2 blocks and turn right on
Brunswick

Old friends Dianna Hrysko and Mary Allen wanted to run a B&B. So, like others before them, they bought a large, old house loaded with potential. It was built in 1907 in the solid Edwardian mode – no Victorian excesses here. What the house may have lacked in whimsy, Dianna and Mary made up for in the cheerful country decor.

On the third floor, each took a room to decorate. Mary's Room is country, with wide pine plank floors painted hunter green with hooked rugs. The bathroom has a clawfoot tub and watermelon-bordered wallpaper. Dianna's room is Victorian. It's done in bright pinks, yellows and white with a modern bathroom. Both rooms have double beds.

The other four rooms are on the second floor and one – Juliet's – has its own *balcony*. Its colours are cream and rose, and the iron-and-brass bed is queen-size. The other rooms are decorated in like manner.

All have private bathrooms.

Breakfast, when I was there, was laid out buffet-style, in generous quantities, and the quality was first-rate. Everything in the fruit cup was at its peak. There were scones, muffins, bagels and fruit breads. Tasty Mennonite sausage. A tempting selection of cheeses. And probably a few things I've missed. Mary tells me they now serve a full breakfast so yours might be a little different. But I have no doubt it will be good.

50

- Deacon House -

*Deacon House is a mix of
generous spirit and spirited decor.*

Flint's Inn Bed & Breakfast

Peter and Gerri Flint
220 Mornington St.
Stratford, ON N5A 5G5
519-271-9579

Best time to call: anytime
Season: all year
Rates: S $50, double $60-80
(no taxes)
Restrictions: no sleeping facilities
for young children, no smoking,
no guests' pets
Facilities: 3 bedrooms (2 twin-
bedded, 1 double); 1 suite (king
and double); 2 bathrooms (1
private with combined shower/
tub, 1 shared by guests with
combined shower/tub); living
room for guests; bedrooms air-
conditioned
Parking: in triple drive
Breakfast: full
Location: see first Stratford entry
Directions: from Ontario St, turn
north on Waterloo. Go 5 blocks.
Turn right onto Mornington and
immediately left onto Duke. Park
in first drive on right

If you're wondering about the word "inn," don't. This *is* a B&B, home to its retired hosts, Peter and Gerri Flint. As is often the case, I wanted a look around before deciding to stay. Gerri's the one who answered my knock on the door. Some hosts are a bit wary when you turn up out of nowhere instead of phoning first. But Gerri was so agreeable, that my travel companion and I almost decided to stay without seeing the rooms.

Interestingly, the house was originally an Ontario cottage. But in 1868, well after it was built, the owner added a second storey with mansard roof. Large windows and elaborate cornices attest to its heritage. Upstairs, three bedrooms share a bath, but the Flints rent only two rooms at a time. The Blue Room's white casement windows and white-painted iron twin beds are in bold contrast with the navy wallpaper. The marble fireplace is probably the first thing you'll notice in Grey Room, also with twin beds. Its colour scheme is burgundy and

pink, and the wallpaper's grey. In the double-bedded Peach Room, there are more casement windows, one with a window seat.

The contemporary suite, with private bathroom, is part of a recent addition over the garage at the back. It has double and king-size beds and lots of comfortable seating. Inside *and* outside. It's just a step out to a screened-in porch.

For breakfast, Gerri does a variation on eggs Benedict. But you may get quiche and coffee cake or tried-and-true ham and eggs. After breakfast, we went out to Peter's workshop, where he refinishes antiques. His specialty is old windows which end up as mirrors. You'll probably notice some throughout the house. If you like them, he may even have a couple for sale.

— Flints Inn Bed & Breakfast —

This house was originally built in the Ontario cottage style in the first half of the nineteenth century. The second storey, and mansard roof, were added in 1868.

Spindles

Susan and Roger Erb
180 Elizabeth St.
Stratford, ON N5A 4Z3
519-273-6393

Best time to call: 9 AM to 9 PM
Season: all year
Rates: S $85-110, D $95-120 (plus GST) enquire about off-season rates
Cards: MC
Restrictions: children 8 and older welcome, smoking on verandah, no guests' pets
Facilities: 3 bedrooms (2 queen, 1 king, can be twins); 3 en suite bathrooms (2 shower only, 1 shower/tub); wall air-conditioners in bedrooms; main floor for guests; mobile telephone
Parking: off-street for 3 cars
Breakfast: full
In residence: one outside smoker
Location: residential area within 10 mins walk to city centre
Directions: from Hwy 7/8 (Ontario St), turn N on Waterloo St and cross river. Turn right (east) onto Elizabeth St

Having handled numerous inquiries from Stratford's tourists for several years as part of her job, host Susan Erb had a finely-tuned sense of what people wanted in B&B, which she's now set out to provide in her own. Susan and husband, Roger, have renovated this century-old Dutch colonial home especially for B&B and, I'd say, she's got it right.

Outside, there's a private furnished patio for guests along with an in ground pool. And inside, there's a comfortable common area plus three guest bedrooms, upstairs, each decorated with flair. One thing Susan learned is that there aren't enough rooms with separate beds for friends to share. So the Derby Room has twin beds (which Susan will happily make up as a king when required). As well, the decor has more of a masculine feel, than the usual feminine, with burgundy, dark green and butter-scotch, lightened up with cream trim. No frills in here.

Next door, however, the queen-bedded Cherub Room is decidedly feminine with an iron-and-brass antique bed, enhanced by a lace valance above the headboard. Wine, pink and soft cream are the colours and the room comes complete with cherubs cavorting near the ceiling. Very pretty. The Anniversary is the largest (and most expensive). There's a queen-size bed, separate seating in the oversize dormer window and a large, elevated area containing a sink, shower, Jacuzzi *and* gas fireplace. Romance anyone? (The toilet *is* behind closed doors.)

Next morning, breakfast is above the ordinary. Always a fruit course and then something like coddled eggs with parsley and chives, or rum-and-raisin French toast. And throughout your stay, Susan provides little extras that you'll appreciate – an early morning coffee basket at your door. A turn down and towel service in the evening. And lots of friendly advice about what to see and do – she's very well practised.

- Spindles B&B -

Lots of little extras here. You'll be looked after in style.

Blue Shutter Guest House

Mary Lou and John Appleton
P.O. Box 135
106 William St. S.
Tavistock, ON N0B 2R0
519-655-2643
1-888-873-3858

Best time to call: anytime
Season: all year
Rates: S $75, D $80-90
(no taxes). Off-season $65
Cards: VISA and MC
Restrictions: children over 12 welcome, smoking on porch only, no guests' pets
Facilities: 3 bedrooms (1 twin-bedded, 1 queen, 1 king); 3 private bathrooms (2 en suite with combined shower/whirlpool tub, 1 private-use with tub and shower); family room with fireplace and porch for guests; air conditioners in bedrooms
Parking: plenty on site
Breakfast: full
Location: 15 min E of Stratford
Directions: take Hwy 59 through town. Turn at William St S

So what do you do when the last of your children leaves home? With a beautiful Italianate-style Victorian house on which you've lavished much attention, perhaps you should consider B&B. Which is exactly what Mary Lou and John Appleton have done.

Driving up, you *almost* think you're entering the world of Trisha Romance – the artist who does those evocative portraits of Ontario's fine old houses. The red gravel lane takes you past a gazebo-style porch on the side and you park out back surrounded by perennial gardens featuring a rose arbour, pond and waterfalls.

By the time outgoing host Mary Lou Appleton greeted me, I had no doubt that I wanted her B&B in this book – it was *that* fast. The room I favoured has an en suite bathroom with whirlpool tub, mahogany king-size bed, and is decorated in soft, neutral colours with lace curtains. There is also a private deck off this room overlooking the gardens. It was reserved, so I stayed in the room with a queen bed which has a bath close by. It's the original bathroom with an old-fashioned tub and modern shower. The third room has twin walnut poster beds and an en suite bathroom.

Mary Lou provides a full breakfast in either the formal dining room or the breakfast room which has a full view of the gardens. I learned at breakfast (fresh fruit including Kiwi and a delicious quiche) that the other guests were there for the Stratford theatre, just 15 minutes away by car. Afterwards, the husband of one of the couples took me aside when he heard about my book, and confessed he'd been miffed at his wife for reserving a B&B outside Stratford. He wanted me to know, now that he'd been to the Blue Shutter Guest House, he wouldn't have it any other way.

- Blue Shutter Guest House -

When you pull into the red gravel drive here you feel like you're entering the world of Trisha Romance.

Denwycke House

Patricia and John Hunter
203 Main St. East
Grimsby, ON L3M 1P5
905-945-2149 (Fax: 945-6272)
E-mail:
johnhunter@compuserve.com

Best time to call: morning/evening
Season: all year
Rates: S $95, D $115 (includes GST) Off season rates available
Cards: VISA/MC
Restrictions: no children under 10, no smoking, no guests' pets
Facilities: 2 suites (1 king, 1 king or twin) each with en suite 4-piece bathroom and private sitting room; (living room for guests); central air, TV, phone and data port for computer hook-up in rooms
Parking: ample
Breakfast: full
Location: on Niagara wine route, a few blocks from Grimsby's business section
Directions: from the QEW, take Bartlett St. exit south to Main St E in Grimsby. Turn right and look for 200 foot low stone fence across front of B&B

Denwycke hosts Pat and John Hunter have been doing B&B longer than anyone else in this book. In fact, they ran the popular Blue Spruces in Ottawa for 14 years before their recent move to Grimsby. Faithful readers will know how much I liked the Hunters' Ottawa B&B, and now they've outdone themselves. Look what's on offer.

Built in the 1840s, Denwycke is a fine example of the architecture of its period. Pull into the circular drive and you'll notice some interesting details, like the classic front porch and deep bracketed eaves. Once inside, the show continues, with chandeliers, high ceilings, and ornate woodwork.

Upstairs, you'll have a choice of two suites with en suite bathrooms and separate sitting rooms; each with a sofa, two comfortable chairs, plus a TV, phone and desk. The Van Duser Suite, named after the United Empire Loyalist descendants who built the house, is bright and sunny with pale yellow wallpaper containing rose and green accents. The king-size bed's headboard originated in Paisley, Scotland about 1830. The Barbour Suite is named after the prominent Grimsby family who owned the house for forty years until the Hunters bought it. Pat has decorated this suite around a garden-room theme with green-and-white ivy wallpaper. Its sitting room has a view of the fountain and rose garden and the bedroom has two four-poster, extra long, twin beds which can be converted into a king size.

Next morning, there'll be much to admire in the richly furnished dining room. And much to enjoy at table. I've smacked my lips over Pat's Belgian pecan waffles, but you could just as easily have crepes or blueberry pancakes. After, you'll find lots of interesting places to explore in and around Grimsby. Architecture and history buffs will find it interesting to visit the nearby remains of a century-old summer community on Lake Ontario.

- Denwycke House -

Two beautifully-furnished private suites await you at Denwyck, along with two most agreeable hosts and a memorable breakfast.

Willow Manor

Jack and Lyn Edwards
408 Willow Rd.
Guelph, ON N1H 6S5
519-763-3574

Best time to call: anytime
Season: all year
Rates: S or D $70-100 (plus GST)
Restrictions: children over 12 welcome, no smoking, no guests' pets
Facilities: 5 bedrooms (2 king, 1 queen, 2 double beds); 4 bathrooms (3 en suite with combined shower/Jacuzzi, 1 with Jacuzzi shared by guests); living room for guests; in-ground pool
Parking: plenty on site
Breakfast: full on Sunday, otherwise continental
Location: 45-minute drive west of Metro Toronto outskirts
Directions: from Hwy 401 take Hwy 6 north 13 kms to Willow Rd. Turn left. Willow Manor is 2nd house on left

In researching previous editions of this book, I'd pinpointed one city ripe for a good B&B. It had a university, good restaurants, a well-to-do population, and an historic past. That city was Guelph. Torontonians Jack and Lyn Edwards saw the gap as well, thought it was a community that suited their needs – pharmaceutical executive Jack could retire while Lyn commuted to her marketing job in Toronto – and dove in.

Willow Manor is an 1860s Georgian-style stone house set back on a small estate property. When the Edwards happened upon it, its architectural bones were flawless, but the decor was dated. Now, from the moment you walk in, you're knocked out. Not only by the French-country decor but by the thoughtful extra touches. Fresh flowers everywhere. Thick white terry robes in the rooms. The fluffiest of duvets on the beds. Cedar-lined closets. Small fridges stocked with mix and mineral water. Tiled bathroom floors that are *heated*. The list goes on.

As for the guest bedrooms, they're all *exquisite* – their decor sets the standard for this book. If you want large, book the Master Bedroom. It shares a bath with one other room, and both have working fireplaces. A third room, on the second floor, has its own bathroom as does the capacious Loft which can be reached from inside, but which also has its own outside entrance. It has a king-size bed and features a giant Jacuzzi. The fifth room, near the front entrance downstairs, is a favourite of business-types. It has its own bathroom and fireplace with a queen-size bed.

The Edwards hobbies are gardening and cooking. You'll see the results of the former when you arrive (even with snow on the ground!) and taste the results of the latter when you leave. On Sundays, breakfast might be warm fruit compote with Amaretto followed by Belgian waffles – that's what we had. Even the weekday continental is reputed to be an indulgence.

~ Willow Manor ~

A flawless restoration and a B&B that's full of thoughtful extra touches.

Esperanza Farms Bed & Breakfast

John R. Garrett
4272 Watson Rd.
Puslinch, ON N0B 2J0
519-763-6385 (Fax: 837-2211)
E-mail: john.garrett@sympatico.ca

Best time to call: 9 AM-9 PM
Languages: a little Spanish/French
Season: all year
Rates: S $45, D $60, Suite $85
(taxes incl.)
Cards: VISA/MC
Restrictions: children over 12
welcome, smoking outside only,
enquire about guests' pets
Facilities: 3 bedrooms (3 queen);
1 en suite bath (tub only), 1 bath
shared by guests (shower/tub), 1
main-floor bath shared with host
(shower/tub); sitting room and
kitchen for guests; central air;
guest office; space in barn for
guests' horses
Breakfast: full
In residence: Sasha, Rocky &
Hannibal, the cats (never in guest
area)
Location: 10 mins S of Guelph,
between Guelph Line & Hwy 6
Directions: map supplied

When driving up the lane to Esperanza Farms, look to your right and you'll notice an attractively landscaped pond with some lawn chairs set up for guests to enjoy the antics of the white Peking ducks which live there year round. Surrounded by gardens and farm land, it's hard to believe you're just ten minutes from Guelph and less than an hour from Toronto. Stressed-out city folk can land here and immediately start to slow down. Business travellers can also enjoy the countryside living, while having access to a guest office with phone and fax. Naturally, long distance charges apply.

Host John Garratt produces hay on the property, boards a few horses and runs the B&B. His guest bedrooms are all upstairs. Refinished pine floors are found throughout most of the house. The rooms are nicely decorated without a lot of clutter though you may come across some of John's personal belongings stored discreetly in the rooms. All have queen-size beds. Two of the large comfortably-furnished bedrooms share

a couple of bathrooms; one on the same floor and one shared with John on the first. The piece-de-resistance here, though, is the large master suite with walkout balcony and private bathroom. It offers views over the fields and an atmosphere of airy grandeur.

The next morning, the gregarious John, serves up a Canadian-style breakfast in the formal dining room. Main dishes include pancakes and sausages or scrambled eggs with bacon and hash browns. Just off the dining room is where you'll find the handy guest kitchen with fixings for tea and coffee. John doesn't mind if you want to prepare light meals here, but for a treat you'll want to try one of the several good restaurants nearby.

Besides being a place to just relax, Esperanza Farms is central to lots of activity. Picturesque villages and antique shops abound. Mohawk Raceway and African Lion Safari are both nearby. Not to mention golf courses and the Glen Eden Ski Hill.

— Esperanza Farms B&B —

*Relax in style at this lovely old
stone farm house with pond.*

Haddo House

Diana and Ron Kennedy
107 Aberdeen Ave.
Hamilton, ON L8P 2P1
905-524-0071

Best time to call: anytime
Season: all year
Rates: S or D $75-105 (no taxes)
Restrictions: no children, smoking outside, no guests' pets
Facilities: 2 bedrooms; 2 bathrooms (1 with tub; 1 with combined shower/tub); den shared by guests
Parking: double drive off Bay St
Breakfast: full
In residence: Max, the toy poodle (easily removed if you're allergic)
Location: within walking distance of downtown
Directions: take Aberdeen exit from Hwy. 403. Continue on Aberdeen to flashing yellow light at Bay St S. Haddo House is on southwest corner

Was it or wasn't it? Haddo House, named after the son of a Scottish lord, *may* have been designed by renowned American architect Frank Lloyd Wright. (A couple of local architects think it's possible.) Or it may not. Regardless, there are some arresting architectural details: a grand central hall with an impressive staircase and several rooms radiating from its perimeter; original curved glass windows; and an entrance foyer with double doors containing beautiful bevelled glass.

The Kennedys are gracious hosts, suiting the spirit of Haddo House located in an upscale residential area of Hamilton. Ron's a retired school superintendent and it's Diana's flair you see at work throughout the house. The den, to your right as you enter, has hunter green walls, and Diana's used the Kennedy tartan on the two wing chairs and sofa. Here you're welcome to watch TV or read.

The second-floor guest bedroom is something to behold. Just beyond the canopy bed, covered with antique linens and lace, an ornate archway frames a small sitting area. All is white and blue, and you can gaze dreamily at the back gardens through the lace-curtained window. It has its own private bathroom next door.

Another air-conditioned bedroom on the third floor is decorated in similar fashion. But with dormer walls sloping from a 10-foot ceiling, it has more of a cottage-like ambiance. Its private bathroom is on the same floor.

There's a nice touch here. As soon as it's warm enough, Diana starts line-drying her white cotton sheets. If you have a hard time remembering what it's like to sleep with sheets smelling of fresh air, it's worth the visit to bring back those memories. And if you're a child of the clothes dryer, go, find out what you missed.

Haddo House

Haddo House has lots going for it – romantic white lace bedrooms, distinctive architecture, a ritzy neighbourhood and, best of all, line-dried white cotton sheets.

Blaney House

Betty and Brock Blaney
177 Victoria St.
P.O. Box 302
Niagara-on-the-Lake, ON
L0S 1J0
905-468-5362

Best time to call: anytime
Season: all year
Rates: S or D $95-100
(no taxes)
Restrictions: not suitable for children, no smoking, no guests' pets
Facilities: 3 bedrooms (1 twin-bedded *or* king, 2 queen); 3 bathrooms (2 en suite with combined shower/tub, 1 en suite with shower only); no common area for guests; central air
Parking: 2 cars side-by-side in driveway, with one parked behind
Breakfast: full
Location: a 2-hour drive from Toronto. Blaney House is downtown, within walking distance of theatres
Directions: from the main street, turn north on Victoria St. Go to 3rd house on west side

Built circa 1816, Blaney House was constructed of clapboarded frame. It's a storey-and-a-half colonial-style with two end-gables. The front door is crowned by a plain transom light, and inside you'll find thick pine-plank floors and most of the original plaster, wood trim and windows – including the glass. Like many before (and many, no doubt, to follow), Toronto-dwellers Betty and Brock Blaney liked the town and its architecture, and retired here in 1989.

Blaney House has a good set-up for two couples travelling together. There's no lounge for guests, but two couples do have *exclusive* use of the second floor and both rooms have spacious sitting areas. The Victorian Room has a king or twin beds (your choice) and is decorated in green and red with white wicker. The Colonial Room is in lighter shades of green and peach with a brass queen-size bed and decorative fireplace. Both have sloped ceilings and en suite bathrooms.

The third room, with private bath, is off the main-floor dining room. It's done in soft yellow with a smattering of royal blue. A cream-coloured partial canopy, attached to the wall, provides a frame for the bed.

In the dining room, dark walnut and cherry antiques provide a lavish backdrop for the silver, crystal and white linen. Here, breakfast often starts with fruit juice and croissants and from there it varies. Perhaps kiwi-topped melon wedges chased with a zucchini frittata. Or herb tea biscuits with apple wedges, followed by Belgian waffles topped with yogurt and fruit. In good weather, Betty sometimes serves breakfast on the back terrace overlooking the gardens and pool.

- Blaney House -

Breakfast here is a fanciful affair and it's not just because of the antique-furnished dining room, bright with crystal, silver and white linen.

Heron House

Katherine Heron
P.O. Box 249
356 Regent Street
Niagara-on-the-Lake, ON
L0S 1J0
905-468-4553

Best time to call: anytime
Besides English: French
Season: all year
Rates: S $90, D $105
(no taxes); winter rates available
Restrictions: children welcome
(Oct through April), no smoking,
no guests' pets
Facilities: 2 bedrooms with
private bathrooms (both with
combined shower/tub); sun room
for guests
Parking: off street
Breakfast: extended continental
In residence: teen-age Kate;
Smudge, the Dalmation
Location: see first NOTL entry.
Heron House is 4 blocks south of
downtown; it's about a 15-minute
walk to the Shaw Festival
Theatre
Directions: turn south off main
street (Queen) at Regent St

From what I've seen, you're unlikely to have a bad experience in any B&B in Niagara-on-the-Lake. Even the ones *not* mentioned here are well above the average in the province. And a few set the highest standards. For example, Heron House. Katherine Heron lives in a beautifully restored 1870 Victorian house. She built an addition in modified Victorian style several years ago. And that's where you'll find the B&B quarters.

If privacy is what you're looking for, this B&B is a good bet. Each bedroom has a bright en suite bathroom, and the dining area for guests is separate from the family section. The romantic bedrooms are all white linen and wicker, with pretty floral wallpapers. Windows are dormer-style and each room has two Victorian brass and white-painted iron beds – one double and one three-quarter. Bed linens are white cotton with lace duvets. Downstairs, I was especially enamoured of the sun room's brightly-hued Sanderson wallpaper. The breakfast served here is what Katherine calls "extended continental," since it includes an omelet, frittatas, soufflés or Belgian waffles, along with caramelized fruits, yogurt and cheeses. Whether breakfasting inside, or outside on the deck, you'll have a country-like view of the lawn and ravine beyond.

— Heron House —

The rooms here have romantic inclinations. Dorner windows. White linen and lace with pretty floral wallpapers.

Hummingbird Hill Cottage

Lee and Beth Alma
P.O. Box 1213
21 Prideaux St.
Niagara-on-the-Lake, Ont.
L0S 1J0
905-468-4635

Best time to call: anytime
Season: April through October
Rates: S or D $70 (no taxes)
Restrictions: limited smoking, no guests' pets
Facilities: 3 bedrooms (1 double, 2 twin-bedded) 2 bathrooms shared with hosts (1 on main floor with combined shower/tub, 1 2-piece on second floor); living room for guests; air conditioners in bedrooms
Parking: beside house
Breakfast: full
Location: see first NOTL entry. Hummingbird Hill Cottage is within walking distance of downtown and theatres
Directions: from the main street (Queen) turn north (towards the lake) on King St. Turn left on Prideaux St

A white picket fence and English garden surround this 1820 salt-box-style house with full-length verandah. And at $70 a night for two it's pretty good value, but only for Niagara-on-the-Lake, which can be *very* expensive. You *do* share the two bathrooms, one on each floor, with hosts, Beth and Lee Alma, but they're very discreet. (Besides, at this B&B you get your own personal bath mat.)

Two of the guest bedrooms are upstairs. The one with the four-poster double bed is my favourite. It's a little larger than the others and has its own deck overlooking a back garden planted with pear, apple and cherry trees. The other upstairs room has two sleigh beds, and a window seat with a view of the front gardens.

These rooms were taken, so we stayed in the downstairs room to the right of the front entrance, which has two pineapple beds. The main-floor bathroom is the one with the shower, so in the morning we scooted in and out pretty quickly, since its door is partly on view from the dining room, where some early-risers were waiting for breakfast.

We had our breakfast with the other guests – and the Almas. We learned that Beth's a retired teacher and husband Lee is semi-retired. It's not often B&B hosts sit down with you for breakfast, though they'll often join you for coffee after. This was a homey change.

70

Hummingbird Hill Cottage

This sweet little cottage, set well back from the street, represents pretty good B&B value – for Niagara-on-the-Lake.

The Saltbox

Carol Gray
P.O. Box 773
223 Gate St.
Niagara-on-the-Lake, ON
L0S 1J0
905-468-5423
E-mail: Willgray@region.net

Best time to call: after 10 AM
Season: all year
Rates: S or D $80 (no taxes)
Restrictions: children over 12 welcome, no smoking, no guests' pets
Facilities: 2 bedrooms (2 double); 1 bathroom shared only by guests (shower/tub); sitting room for guests; central air
Parking: in drive or legally overnight on street
Breakfast: full
In residence: Jake, the tabby
Location: see first NOTL entry. The Saltbox is easy walking distance to downtown and theatres
Directions: turn south off main street (Queen) at Gate St. The Saltbox is half a block south

If you're like me, when you travel B&B, you occasionally find yourself envious of some hosts' homes or lifestyles. Well, I'm envious of The Saltbox. And of Carol Gray and husband, David Willett, who found this beautiful old home, and moved from Toronto a few years ago. Carol's the full-time host and David's an engineer who specializes in hydro-electric projects around the world.

This house is *old;* over one hundred and seventy years old. It's an early Niagara saltbox, renovated in 1973 by Paul Johns, a local designer. He opened up the rooms but left the old beamed ceilings and pine floors. I particularly liked the stairs. With their higher-than-usual steps and primitive bannister, they're part of the character of this place.

The two cosy guestrooms and shared bathroom are on the second floor. So be prepared to step lively up those stairs! Both bedrooms have sloping ceilings and double beds. One is done in white, pink and grey, with a white wicker rocker. The other has floral wallpaper and a Jenny Lind bed. You'll also find a dressing table made of a buck-board buggy seat on top of an old treadle sewing machine stand. The wall-to-wall carpeting in both rooms is in a bright zig-zag pattern reminiscent of rag rugs.

Next morning, after breakfast, you may want to stroll about the large English-style garden out back where David's put in an ornamental pond. It comes complete with fountain, water lilies and goldfish.

- The Saltbox -

Beamed ceilings, pine floors, sloped ceilings and primitive stairs – all have been lovingly restored in this 170-year-old house.

73

Old Port Dalhousie Hayocks

Ron and Barbara Nunn
43 Ann Street
St. Catharines, ON L2N 5E9
905-934-7106 (phone/fax)

Best time to call: anytime
Season: mid-April to Nov (other times by request)
Rates: S $70-75, D $85-90, Suite $150 (no taxes) Enquire about off-season rates
Restrictions: children over 12 OK, no smoking, no guests' pets
Facilities: 1 suite (king) with 2 bathrooms (1 shower only, 1 tub only); 2 rooms (1 twin-bedded, 1 queen); 2 en suite bathrooms (1 shower only, 1 shower/tub); solarium with phone for guests, air conditioning in bedrooms, fax available at cost
Parking: off-street for 3 cars
Breakfast: full
In residence: occasionally 2 "grand-dogs" visit: (never in guest quarters)
Location: Niagara Region
Directions: exit QEW at 7th St and go N to Lakeshore. Turn right, drive 6 km to Ann St. Turn left

Beautifully landscaped with a cobblestone-look cement drive, and with over 120 feet of Lake Ontario shoreline, you know you're onto something special as soon as you drive into Haycocks B&B. Hosts Ron and Barbara Nunn have done much of the restoration work themselves on this English cottage-style stucco home built in 1860.

Now, let's cut right to the chase. For sure, the guest bedrooms at Haycocks B&B are very attractive and comfortable. Both have en suite bathrooms and both have views of Lake Ontario. But if you can afford it, spring for the suite. I know it sounds expensive at $150 a night ($125 in the winter). But attentive readers will know I always look for good value. And I say this one is good value.

So what makes the suite so special? Well, for starters, there are his and her bathrooms. One has a dressing area and sunken tub with skylight overhead, separated by a glass brick wall from the rest of the bathroom. The other is a four-piece with shower and tub. Then there's the 1820s mahogany four-poster queen-size bed with hand-carved pineapples, dressed in Sanderson fabrics. It faces a gas fireplace with wood mantel and slate hearth. Ornate crown mouldings highlight the ceiling. Wide pocket doors open to the sitting area with two overstuffed armchairs and matching hassock. From there, on a clear day, your view through the large casement windows is of the distant Toronto skyline. And most evenings you can put your feet up and watch a spectacular sunset.

The next morning, breakfast consists of OJ, fresh fruit, perhaps a hot egg dish or some variation on pancakes, or French toast, often with bacon or sausage and herbed potatoes. After, you could get to know Old Port Dalhousie which, even though part of St. Catharines, is village-like with several restaurants, interesting shops and a boat harbour. It's also famed for its rowing regattas but you'd better book well in advance for those.

- Hayocks -

A village atmosphere, plus more than 100 feet of Lake Ontario shore with a view of Toronto's skyline.

Beaconsfield

Bernie and Katya McLoughlin
38 Beaconsfield Ave.
Toronto, ON M6J 3H9
416-535-3338
E-mail: beacon@idirect.com

Best time to call: morning/
evening
Season: all year
Besides English: Spanish/Slavic;
some French/German
Rates: S $59, D $69, suite $99
(no taxes)
Restrictions: smoking on decks
or verandah; no guests' pets
Facilities: 1 suite (queen and cot)
(private bath combined shower/
tub); 2 bedrooms (1 queen, 1
king *or* twin-bedded); 1 bathroom
shared by guests (combined
shower/tub); common room and
deck for guests; central air
Parking: for 4 cars in drive
Breakfast: full
In residence: Macho, the cat
Location: 4 kms west of Yonge
near Queen/Dufferin. Easy access
to Gardiner Expwy. Half block to
Queen St streetcar
Directions: obtain when booking

If you're looking for something different, Beaconsfield's the place to stay. The whole street's been designated historic. And you'll find a mixture of Portuguese immigrants, and creative types like the McLoughlins. Katya's a film actress and Bernie has his artist's studio behind the house. Several blocks away you'll find the heart of Toronto's artsy Queen Street West strip, lined with funky shops and creative eateries.

The decor here is a shared effort of the McLoughlins; from the murals that Bernie paints on the walls to Katya's off-beat decorating ideas.

The Mexican-themed San Miguel suite on the third floor has its own kitchen, bathroom, living room and deck. The deck, surrounded by a "cactus" fence, is full of plants and strung with colourful lanterns. On a warm summer night, with mariachi music playing (Katya thinks of everything), while sipping a margarita (your contribution), you'd almost think you *were* in Mexico – except for the superb view of Toronto's CN Tower.

The two bedrooms on the second floor share a bathroom decorated with one of Bernie's whimsical murals. Help yourself to bubble bath and candles. By now you won't be surprised to see a wall and ceiling painting of Georgian Bay in one of the bedrooms – the one with the queen-size bed. The other has twins which can be made into a king, and sports a mural of rolling farm country. Most guests end up in the adjoining former kitchen or out on the deck overlooking the garden. You'll find lots of interest – tourist info, magazines, games, books, colour TV, VCR, fridge, microwave, even toys for your children. A big round table encourages socializing, perhaps over a cup of coffee or tea you can make yourself.

Katya serves breakfast in the dining room full of books and paintings. It could be an omelet or a fruit pancake – in season, the fruit's sure to be fresh raspberries or peaches from the backyard.

- Beaconsfield -

For something delightfully different stay at Beaconsfield. Katya's an actress and Bernie's an artist and they live on a street full of Victorian homes that's been designated historic.

Clarence Square

Susan and Garry Walker
13 Clarence Square
Toronto, ON M5V 1H1
416-598-0616 (Fax: 598-4200)

Best time to call: anytime
Season: all year
Rates: S $110-120, D $120-130
(plus GST)
Cards: VISA/MC/AMEX
Restrictions: no small children, teen-agers welcome, smoking outside, no guests' pets
Facilities: 3 bedrooms (1 double, 1 queen, 1 king which can be twins); 3 en suite bathrooms (all with shower/whirlpool tub); main-floor salon for guests; air conditioning; phone in bedrooms; fax and modem available for guest computer (no charge)
Parking: off-street for 3 cars
Breakfast: full
Location: in heart of Toronto's vibrant entertainment district
Directions: from Hwy 401, exit at Yonge St S and go 10 km to Wellington St. Turn W and go 1 km to B&B. From QEW, exit Yonge St N, go 1 km to Wellington St. Turn W. 1 km to B&B

I simply can't imagine a better location for visitors to downtown Toronto than Clarence Square. Not only can you walk to theatres, restaurants, Chinatown and the fashion trendsetters on Queen Street, but you'll have lovely accommodations on a quiet one-block street of restored Victorian townhomes which overlook a small park. Hosts Susan and Garry Walker have done themselves proud.

Inside you'll find a restoration which respects the history of the place but provides all the modern amenities. To the left as you enter, the guest salon is lightly furnished with raspberry-coloured Louis XV armchairs and contrasting loveseat next to the marble fireplace. Beyond, is the dining area with three wicker dining sets offering intimate breakfasts for two.

Upstairs, all three bedrooms have telephones, colour TVs with access to cable, whirlpool tubs in the private bathrooms and individual-control air conditioning and heating systems. The romantic queen-bedded Wellington Room, with wood-burning fireplace, faces the park with a view of the CN Tower beyond. The Simcoe Room has a double brass bed and Canadiana pine armoire. Traditional mahogany furnishings define the York Room. Its king-size bed, dressed with Ralph Lauren linens, can be converted to twins if required. Sliding glass doors take you out to a small ivy-covered balcony.

The next morning, crystal, fine china, white linens, and fresh flowers grace the tables. You'll have a multi-course breakfast with juices, home baking, fresh fruits and a choice of at least two main courses such as Mexican eggs baked in a tortilla or buttermilk pancakes with sauteed apples.

Toronto boosters, Susan and Garry have all sorts of interesting information about what to see and do. They count food, wine and the arts among their interests, so if yours are in common you couldn't have better guides.

- Clarence Square -

This tiny residential oasis in the heart of downtown Toronto is truly a find.

79

The English Corner

Fred and Carol Hansen
114 Bernard Ave.
Toronto, ON M5R 1S3
416-967-6474
Fax: 416-967-9382

Best time to call: 10 AM to 10 PM
Season: all year
Rates: S $70, D $85-90
(no taxes). Minimum two-night
stay on weekends
Restrictions: children over 12
welcome, no smoking, no guests'
pets, no drinking
Facilities: 3 guest bedrooms (1
twin-bedded, 1 double, 1 queen);
2 bathrooms (1 shower/tub, 1
combined shower/tub); living
room for guests; air conditioners
in bedrooms
Parking: in driveway, and hosts'
lot a block away
Breakfast: full
Location: central, 10-minute walk
to U of T
Directions: obtain when booking

If I only had one word to describe this B&B it would be *immaculate*. To keep it that way, hosts Carol and Fred Hansen ask you to remove your shoes at the front door and don a pair of knit slippers. The surroundings here remind you of England – gas fireplace, understated chintzes and cherry wood panelling. Guests may gather round the fire in the living room or, in warmer weather, in the glassed-in porch full of wicker and greenery. There are also a couple of other nooks you can use for a quiet read.

You can hardly ask for a better Toronto location. The English Corner B&B is in The Annex, a quiet residential mid-town neighbourhood full of grand old chestnut trees and large older homes. The subway's a block and a half away and it's a pleasant 15-minute walk to Yorkville and the upscale shopping on Bloor Street.

The three guest bedrooms, on the second and third floors, are simply but attractively decorated. My favourite was the third-floor Brass Room because its white-and-rose colour scheme had a little more pizzaz. Probably the best room for a business person is the Trundle Room (its single bed can convert to twins). Done in blue and grey, it has a desk and phone. The Wicker Room has a queen-size bed with wicker headboard and other wicker furnishings.

You'll have breakfast in the bay-windowed dining room which you enter through bevelled-glass French doors. One day, breakfast might be pancakes, another soufflé, and another French toast.

80

The English Corner

The English Corner's in a desirable central-Toronto neighbourhood and it's immaculate.

Feathers

May Jarvie
132 Wells St.
Toronto, ON M5R 1P4
416-534-1923 or 534-2388

Best time to call: before noon and after 4 PM
Besides English: Dutch/French/some German
Season: all year
Rates: S $50-65, D $65-75, suite S $65, D $75 (no taxes)
Restrictions: no smoking
Facilities: 2 bedrooms (both king *or* twin bedded); 1 en suite bath (shower only), 1 bathroom shared by guests (combined shower/tub), 1 main-floor 2-piece shared with host; 1 suite with private bathroom (shower only); living room shared with host; central air
Parking: half block away
Breakfast: continental
Location: near Bloor/Bathurst
Directions: from Bloor/Bathurst intersection drive north 3 blocks to Dupont. Turn right. Go 2 blocks to Howland. Turn right. Drive one block to Wells. Turn right. Go 1½ blocks to 132

Feathers reflects the whimsical personality of its well-travelled host. Fellow artists will find a kindred spirit here. It's also popular with musicians and laid-back academics.

Host May Jarvie is a sociologist by training, and textile artist by design. Evidence of the latter interest abounds. You'll find chairs occupied by life-size soft-sculpture dolls. An antique tapestry from Afghanistan in the dining room. And batik paintings on cloth spotted here and there. The living room is also home to an intriguing collection of antique Indonesian puppets and Japanese festival dolls. Besides them, the living room's decorated with Oriental rugs, original art (some contemporary, some turn of the century), Victorian furnishings, ivory and bronze figurines from China and India, and a collection of blue-and-white antique china on the fireplace mantel.

Feathers is in The Annex, one of central Toronto's finer neighbourhoods, and home to many students because of its proximity to the University of Toronto. It's a great location if you want to be close to Yorkville and Bloor Street. And the subway is only a five-minute walk away.

Perhaps the prettiest guest bedroom is at the front on the second floor. It has a bay window, antique Japanese chests and Persian carpets. The bed is king-size, but can be switched to twins. There is also a smaller room on this floor with a king-sized bed (or twins) decorated in warm shades of pink and white.

Families and honeymooners, though, would probably like the self-contained studio apartment with private back entrance. More modern than the rest of the house, it's nicely decorated, and a remarkable amount of light streams in, considering it's a basement. There's a queen bed on one side of the room, and a twin on the other.

May puts out a continental breakfast, and she doesn't stint. In season, for example, you'll find mango and raspberries in the fruit cup.

Feathers

Eccentrically entertaining, Feathers captures the host's whimsical personality.

The Mulberry Tree

Paul and Carol Buer
122 Isabella St.
Toronto, ON M4Y 1P1
416-960-5249
E-mail: mulberry@aracnet.net

Best time to call: 10 AM to 4 PM
Languages: French, German
Season: all year
Rates: S $60-65, D $75-80 (no taxes)
Restrictions: smoking outside only, no guests' pets
Facilities: 3 bedrooms (1 king or twin, 2 queen); 2 bathrooms shared (1 shower/tub, 1 shower); sitting area for guests; air conditioning, phone and data port in rooms; fax available
Parking: off-street for 4 cars (some jockeying necessary)
Breakfast: full
In residence: Gulliver, the Great Dane (kept away from guests); Pumpkin, the calico cat
Location: near Yonge & Bloor
Directions: from Hwy 401, take Don Valley Pkwy to Bloor St. Turn right. Drive to Huntley. Turn left. Drive to Isabella. Turn right.

Business travellers take note. Paul and Carol Buer, hosts of The Mulberry Tree, have set up their B&B especially to accommodate your needs. You'll have access to fax, e-mail, a message service and some secretarial services. Plus, in your room, you'll have a desk with a data port for your computer. They'll even handle your take-out dry-cleaning and provide an early breakfast if you need it. Which doesn't mean that tourists won't have a fine time here as well. *They* will find attractively decorated guest bedrooms with robes, slippers and basic toiletries provided.

The decor of the home is very European in feeling, with art, antiques and collectibles picked up by the Buers from around the world. You'll also find interesting photographs here and there, and a dining room that's been turned into a photo studio. Turns out, Paul's a professional photographer. Carol's business is advertising and marketing, and they both work from home.

On the second floor you'll find a large guest room with queen bed plus a single. Done in shades of ochre and terra cotta, its large southfacing bay window lets in lots of light. Two more rooms can be found on the third floor. One has a queen-size bed and the other a king-size that can be made up as twins. Both have touches of mulberry in the decor. Here also is where you'll also find a small guest sitting area (and balcony) with colour TV/VCR, a bar fridge and makings for coffee and tea.

Paul and Carol pride themselves on their breakfasts. One day it might be baked apples and a frittata. Another broiled grapefruit and French crepes. And do try the preserves made from the fruit of the mulberry tree out back. Usually, you'll have breakfast in the open kitchen, but when the weather's balmy, you can have it outside in the intimate plant-filled courtyard with ivy-covered wall.

— the Mulberry Tree —

A thoughtful set-up for business travellers, but tourists will love it here too.

85

Orchard View

Donna and Ken Ketchen
92 Orchard View Blvd.
Toronto, ON M4R 1C2
416-488-6826

Best time to call: anytime
Season: all year
Rates: S $60, D $70-75 (no taxes)
Restrictions: older children welcome, no smoking, no guests' pets
Facilities: 2 bedrooms (1 twin-bedded, 1 queen); 2 bathrooms (1 shared with hosts separate tub/shower, 1 en suite combined shower/tub); central air
Parking: for 2 cars in backyard
Breakfast: full
In residence: Schubert, the cat
Location: short walk to Yonge and Eglinton
Directions: one block north of Eglinton, one block west of Yonge (obtain precise directions when booking)

Orchard View B&B is home to Donna and Ken Ketchen. If you stay there, you're just a couple of blocks away from Toronto's bustling Yonge/Eglinton area of shops and restaurants. And the subway's close by, making it convenient for getting around without a car – a good idea considering Toronto's traffic congestion.

There's another good thing about Orchard View. With most B&Bs, the bathroom's shared with other guests. It goes with the territory. True B&B afficionados don't mind it at all. But in a place like Toronto, there seems to be a higher-than-usual demand for private bathrooms. So, if you want a private bathroom, book the queen-bedded room on the third floor. It's decorated in quiet good taste with matching spread and cushions in shades of blue.

The twin-bedded room, on the second floor, has its own entrance into a large, well-appointed bathroom. Though shared with the hosts, it's *almost* like having your own. (Donna and Ken keep their toiletries hidden away, and they have another bathroom for themselves on the main floor.) This room also has a sun room, attractively furnished for reading and relaxing.

In the morning, Donna serves breakfast home-style in the middle of the large kitchen. Or, in nicer weather, on the walk-out deck. Then all you have to do is put on your walking shoes and set out to explore Toronto.

Orchard View

Orchard View is well-situated in north-central Toronto, just a couple of blocks from the subway.

Ezra Annes House

Mary and Ted Wood
239 Wellington Street
Whitby, ON L1N 5L7
905-430-1653 (tel & fax)
1-800-213-1257

Best time to call: anytime
Besides English: some French
Season: all year
Rates: S or D $75-85 (no taxes)
Restrictions: children over 12
welcome, smoking in garden only
Facilities: 2 bedrooms (1 double,
1 queen); 2 en suite bathrooms
(1 shower only, 1 combined
shower/tub)
Parking: plenty on site
Breakfast: full
In residence: 1 family dog
Location: Whitby is a small town
on the eastern fringes of Toronto.
It's 40 minutes by car or GO-
train to downtown Toronto
Directions: from Hwy 401, take
Hwy 12 exit into Whitby. Drive
north to Hwy 2 (Dundas St).
Turn left (west). Drive 1.5 kms to
Wellington Street. Turn right
(north) to second-last house on
right

For those of you who've never given Whitby a second look, except from the 401 as you zip by, here's a good reason to turn off. Ezra Annes built this Georgian-style house in 1836, and Mary and Ted Wood are only the fourth owners. Not only have the Woods restored the house, they've provided an English country house ambiance. At the back, they've added an airy great room with views of the perennial gardens.

The two guest bedrooms are on the second floor. The largest is the sunny yellow Rose Room furnished in early Canadian pine with a queen-size cannon-ball bed. The windows are dressed with a rose damask and there's a private dressing room leading to a bath with shower.

The Queen Victoria Room has a double antique settler's rope bed adapted for modern comfort, plus an en suite bath.

Mary offers a choice for breakfast. Perhaps apple cinnamon French toast, eggs Benedict or her specialty, apples Wellington. Over breakfast you may be interested to learn Ted is a thriller writer of some note – if you're a fan of the genre, perhaps you'll have read his "Dead in the Water".

After, you might like the idea of a stroll along nearby Lynde Creek. Serious nature-lovers and bird-watchers could take the short drive south to Cranberry Marsh and Thickson Woods on Lake Ontario. Or perhaps you fancy an antique tour of the area – thoughtful, as always, Mary provides a map.

— Ezra Annis House —

Noteworthy nature trails and some of Canada's best bird-watching here. Plus an English country house style B&B.

Five Pines

Theo and Austra Kraumanis
R.R. 1
Baltimore, ON K0K 1C0
905-342-2872

Best time to call: anytime (before 8 AM is best)
Besides English: German
Season: March to Dec
Rates: S $80-95, D $95-110, (no taxes)
Restrictions: enquire about guests' pets
Facilities: 2 bedrooms and a cabin; all with private bath (1 combined shower/tub, 2 shower only); living room for guests; in-ground pool
Parking: plenty on site
Breakfast: full
Location: a few kms north of Cobourg
Directions: obtain when booking

Some refer to Five Pines as Theo's Folly – we all should have follies like this. Years before it was built, Theo, a retired pharmacist from nearby Cobourg, had begun collecting materials from old buildings that faced the wrecker's ball. Bevelled glass doors, old wood, huge beams, thick pine planks from an old factory – all of it was stored in a barn, awaiting a new beginning. The old materials were finally used in 1972, when Five Pines was built with the help of the whole family.

Five Pines is a glorious place, very European in its feeling. Situated on a birch-and-pine-wooded hill, overlooking the rolling Northumberland countryside and Lake Ontario beyond, it could easily win your vote for Best View from a B&B.

It's difficult to decide in which room to stay. You could choose the suite with loft bedroom in the main house, with its own sitting area and fireplace. Or the pretty double with a bird feeder outside its window and a view of the woods. Or the romantic little cabin in the forest by a stream, with its own small kitchen and huge fieldstone fireplace. All have double beds and are decorated with flair and imagination.

You're surrounded by fine paintings and interesting artifacts as you dig into the magnificent spread Austra provides for breakfast: exotic fresh fruits, perhaps mangos and papayas, and something special like bacon buns and crepes. Rumour has it that Theo's about to embark on another folly. I can hardly wait.

Five Pines is decorated with flair and imagination, and has a breathtaking view.

Cornelius White House

Frank and Bonnie Evans
8 Wellington St.
P.O. Box 347
Bloomfield, ON K0K 1G0
613-393-2282
E-mail: cwh@connect.reach.net

Best time to call: anytime
Season: all year
Rates: S $60, D $80 (no taxes)
Restrictions: no smoking
Facilities: 1 suite with private bath (combined shower/tub); 3 bedrooms; 1 private 4-piece bath, 2 private 3-piece bath; living room and lounge for guests; central air
Parking: plenty on site
Breakfast: full
In residence: Kiki, the cat
Location: 20-minute drive south of Belleville
Directions: From Toronto, take Hwy 401 east. Exit at Wooler Rd S to Hwy 33. Continue on to Bloomfield. From Kingston, take Hwy 401 west and Hwy 49 south to Picton, then Hwy 33 to Bloomfield

For Frank and Bonnie Evans, settling in Prince Edward County, after a career in the military, was like coming home. Frank was born in nearby Picton, and for many years his grandfather was Bloomfield's barber. But for others, many are just now discovering the County's small farms, quaint villages, pastoral countryside, and beautiful beaches and sand dunes.

If you insist on a private bathroom, there are five possibilities here. First, the main floor Tweedsmuir suite at the back of the house has its own private bathroom. The colours are cream, blue and rust and there's both a sofa bed and a white iron queen-size bed.

Upstairs, all three rooms have en suite bathrooms. The spacious Centennial Room has queen and double beds and is done in taupe, cream and pink. Its bathroom has a shower only. The Prince Edward Room's bed is queen size and it's decorated with floral prints. The bath includes tub and shower. The Loyalist Room, decorated in British red and blue, offers a king-size bed and a 3-piece (shower only) bathroom.

There's also Herb Cottage behind the house. Dried herbs hang from open rafters, and it's decorated in white, green and yellow. It has a private bathroom with shower, plus kitchen facilities.

Bonnie's written a book of her recipes so you'll find some of her breakfast secrets revealed if you choose to buy it. One of her guests' favourites is salmon quiche with dill sauce, which she serves with orange scones.

— Cornelius White House —

Host Bonnie Evans has published a book of her recipes. One favourite of guests is salmon quiche with dill sauce.

Mallory House

Wayne and Flo Cooper
R.R. 1
Bloomfield, ON K0K 1G0
613-393-3458

Best time to call: anytime
Season: May long weekend to
Labour Day
Rates: S $45, D $60 (no taxes)
Restrictions: children welcome
(8 and older, $10 extra; under 8,
free), smoking on verandah,
enquire about guests' pets
Facilities: 3 bedrooms (2 double,
1 twin); 3 bathrooms (1 shower/
tub, 1 shower only, 1 2-piece on
main floor); living room for
guests; family room shared
Parking: plenty on site
Breakfast: full
In residence: Hobbes, your basic
black dog; Shadow, Tigger and
Spiff, the cats
Location: a 2½-hour drive east of
Toronto
Directions: 2nd house on right,
on Hwy 33 east of Bloomfield
limits, before Mallory Rd sign

After Flo's parents passed on, the Coopers couldn't bear to sell Mallory House. Flo had grown up there so it held many happy memories. And it had been in her family for a hundred years. But it was *so* big. And Flo and her husband, Wayne, already had a place to live. One summer, daughter Stephanie ran it temporarily as a B&B. And then the Coopers began to think, well, maybe *they* would do it: become B&B hosts.

Mallory House has all the right ingredients for a memorable B&B experience: a warm, friendly host family and a beautiful home in a picturesque part of the province. For their own quarters, the Coopers renovated the oldest part at the back – they think it dates back to 1810. The main house, built around 1850, serves as the B&B. There are three attractive bedrooms, overlooking the lawn and surrounding countryside, with an old apple orchard way up yonder.

Pick any room, you'll be happy. The Master Bedroom has a non-working fireplace and a four-poster double bed. The bright and airy Guest Room has twin antique brass beds.

Then there's the West Room, which seems to be a favourite of guests. It has an antique double brass bed. Three walls are painted a pale blue, with a floral print paper on the other. The pine floors are covered with dusty rose rugs.

In the evenings, you're welcome to join the Coopers in front of the fireplace in their family room. The next morning, breakfast is full and could include home-baked scones, cinnamon buns or blueberry muffins.

The Mallory House

Mallory House has all the right ingredients for a memorable B&B experience: a warm, friendly host family and a beautiful home in a picturesque part of the province.

Butler Creek Bed & Breakfast

Ken Bôsher and
Burke Friedrichkeit
RR 7, Hwy 30-202
Brighton, ON K0K 1H0
613-475-1248 (Fax: 475-5267)
E-mail: obbrs@mail.reach.net

Best time to call: 9 AM to 10 PM
Languages: German, French
Season: all year
Rates: S $45-70, D $55-85
(no taxes)
Cards: VISA/MC
Restrictions: no smoking, no guests' pets
Facilities: 5 bedrooms (1 twin-bedded, 3 double, 1 queen); 2 en suite bathrooms (1 shower only, 1 2-piece) 1 shared by guests only (shower/tub); lounge with fireplace for guests; telephone in kitchen
Parking: off-road for 5 cars
Breakfast: full
Location: half-way between Toronto and Kingston
Directions: from Hwy 401, take exit 509 and drive 3 km S on Hwy 30. B&B is on right

Like many big-city folk, Ken Bôsher and Burke Friedrichkeit left it all behind for life in the country. And, like many, they opened a B&B – Butler Creek Bed and Breakfast. What's different is that these two had already run Toronto's Burken Guest House for ten years. So while most hosts pack it in after five to seven years, Ken and Burke are in for the long haul. This time they've picked a convenient location just south of Highway 401 midway between Toronto and Kingston, and close to Presqu'ile Provincial Park, well-known for its superb birding, nature trails and wide sandy beaches.

On Highway 30 just north of town, you'll find Burke and Ken's 1905 Victorian house overlooking their large property's picturesque valley which borders a conservation area. To take full advantage of the panorama of trees and meadows, book the Valley View Suite. It has a private entrance with its own large furnished deck, away from the highway traffic. The suite's large living space has two bed chesterfields and small kitchen with eating area. You'll find a separate queen-bedded room down the hall past the bathroom. As for the bathroom, it has a European-style shower; a sloping tiled bathroom floor with drain, and a shower curtain that can be drawn round.

The other rooms feature decorative touches from Germany (Burke's home country), Australia (Ken's) and Hungary (a good friend's). One guest room, with twin beds, has a small two-piece en suite bathroom and two wing chairs. Another room, painted a pale apricot, has wing chairs, queen-size bed and a pedestal washbasin. The other two have double beds, one with a bay window and the other with a pedestal sink. All four share the large bathroom.

The next morning, you'll find the usual breakfast offerings plus a main dish such as eggs Benedict or apple pancakes – fitting since apples figure large in the fortunes of this town surrounded by apple orchards.

- Butler Creek -

Nearby, you'll find some of Ontario's best beaches and nature trails in Presqu'ile Park; not to mention superb birding.

Essex House

Annette Young and Pat Arato
351 George St,
Cobourg, ON K9A 3M2
905-377-3922 (Fax: 377-8825)

Best time to call: anytime
Season: all year
Rates: S $65, D $75 (no taxes)
enquire about off-season rates
Restrictions: smoking outside
only, no guests' pets
Facilities: 4 bedrooms (1 twin-
bedded, 3 queen); 4 en suite
bathrooms (2 shower only, 2
shower/tub); main floor for
guests; telephone in kitchen plus
outlets in bedrooms, fax and
computer if required
Parking: off-street for 4 cars
Breakfast: full
In residence: Patches, the dog;
cats, Whitey, Ginny & Boy-Boy
Location: 1 hr E of Toronto; 5
min walk to downtown Cobourg
Directions: from Hwy 401, take
exit 474 and travel S about 1½
km on Division St to James St.
Turn right to George St (1 block).
Cross George and park on James
beside B&B

Essex House is late Victorian, a design which usually signals assorted impediments for anyone with a mobility disability. But not here. Hosts Annette Young and Pat Arato, not only offer two main-floor guest bedrooms and a convenient ramp at the side entrance, but one of the rooms has a fully accessible en suite bathroom for wheelchair-users. Besides grab bars and an emergency button, it has a large shower stall with built-in seat. In the cornflower-blue bedroom you'll find comfortable twin beds, an antique dresser, wicker loveseat, and dark hardwood floors offering ease of movement for wheelchairs.

As you might expect there's a story here. Both Annette and Pat have experience with disability issues. Pat, in fact, founded the Pat Arato Aphasia Centre in Toronto (renamed in her honour after she retired). Aphasia refers to the loss of language and accompanying physical impairments usually brought on by a stroke. One of her early patients, from whom she learned much, was a man named Don Hall and it's after him that the room above is named.

The other main floor guest room is not *quite* so accessible – its private-use bathroom is next door, but it's an excellent choice for folks who can't take the stairs. The Garden Room, as it's called, is a cosy queen-bedded room decorated in teal blue with two sets of windows overlooking the gardens and bird-feeders.

Upstairs, you'll find the other two guest bedrooms. Both are large, beds are queen-size, bathrooms are private and furnishings are a mix of antique and new. The Rose Room has a plush fitted carpet and the Peach Room's bathroom is decorated with circa 1940s wallpaper recovered from the basement.

Breakfast the next morning will feature all the fixings, including eggs-any-style if you like. But the specialty of the house are Palacsinta, Hungarian pancakes filled with cream cheese – my choice, without question.

Essex House -

*Friendly hosts, private bathrooms and one room that's **completely** wheelchair accessible.*

Mackechnie House

Cathryn Thompson and
Ian Woodburn
173 Tremaine St.
Cobourg, ON K9A 2Z2
905-372-6242
E-mail: BandB@eagle.ca

Best time to call: anytime
Season: all year
Rates: S $55-85, D $60-90 (plus GST)
Cards: AMEX
Restrictions: enquire about children, smoking outside, no guests' pets
Facilities: 3 bedrooms (1 double, 2 queen); 1 en suite bath (shower/tub), 1 shared by guests (shower only); two sitting areas for guests; phone available
Parking: off-street
Breakfast: full
In residence: teen son, Rory; dog and cat live in host's quarters;
Location: 1¼ hrs E of Toronto
Directions: From Hwy 401, take Burnham St exit and go S. At lights, turn left on William. Drive S to King St. Turn right. Go 2 blocks to Tremaine. Turn left.

Breakfast alert! For those of you who search out great B&B breakfasts, make sure you book a stay at Mackechnie House. Host Cathryn Thompson's trade is catering, and look what she dishes out. No plain fruit here. Rather, caramelized mango, poached pears with yogurt, or bananas baked with brown sugar and rum. And the main course? Could be scrambled eggs with brie and sauteed mushrooms with chives, accompanied by peameal bacon and cranberry chutney, with English crumpets to round things out. You get the picture.

The rest of what's offered here won't disappoint either. This 1843-built home has been called by a local historian the most interesting example of Greek revival architecture in Ontario. Cathryn's partner, Ian Woodburn, has done a lot of the restoration. You enter through the large doorway to find yourself in a grand entrance hall with the guest drawing room to the left and dining room to the right. Go up the wide staircase and you'll find yourself in another guest sitting area in the room-sized hall, off which you'll find the guest rooms – spacious with high ceilings and beautifully decorated. Nearby, there's a discreet utility area with bar-fridge and a wide selection of tourist information.

One bedroom, done in soft aqua and rose, features a queen-sized four poster bedroom suite which has been in Ian's family for four generations. There's also a non-working fireplace with a unique surround of coloured foil flowers behind glass. The en suite bathroom has a shower and tub. The other two rooms share a bathroom and are equally pretty; one is done English-country-style with a mahogany four-poster queen-size bed. The other is done in green toile de Jouy with cream accents and has a double bed.

And there's something else – all rooms have particularly comfortable mattresses. In fact, Cathryn's even been known to arrange for smitten guests to purchase a mattress directly from the manufacturer!

- MacKechnie House -

A gracious host, exceptional quarters and outstanding breakfasts.

Victoria View

John and Jayne Duncan
216 Church St.
Cobourg, ON K9A 3V9
905-372-3437

Best time to call: anytime
Season: all year
Rates: S $50, D $65-75 (no taxes)
Restrictions: smoking on verandah only, no guests' pets
Facilities: 3 bedrooms (1 twin-bedded, 1 double, 1 queen); 1 bathroom shared only by guests (combined shower/tub); 1 private bathroom (combined shower/tub); living room for guests; air conditioner on 3rd floor
Parking: on street (legal overnight)
Breakfast: full
In residence: 1 smoker (sun room and verandah only)
Location: an hour's drive east of Toronto
Directions: from Hwy 401 take exit 474 (Hwy 45) south to King St downtown. Turn left. Go 2 blocks to Church. Turn right

John and Jayne Duncan were knocked out by Cobourg's considerable charms. (And they aren't the only ones. The Globe and Mail newspaper has twice touted Cobourg as one of the eight best communities in Canada in which to live and do business.) The Duncans decided to leave Toronto's trendy Cabbagetown behind for life in a small town.

The Duncan's home, Victoria View (so-named because of its location across from Victoria Park), is just a block or so from the beach and Lake Ontario in one direction, and downtown's 19th-century streetscape in another.

The three guest bedrooms are all on the second floor. The one with en suite bath has a queen-size bed decorated with Waverley prints in rose, blue and yellow. Its bathroom has a 6-foot clawfoot tub, pedestal sink and separate shower stall. The other two share a bathroom down the hall. The largest is the twin-bedded blue-and-white front room. Jabot curtains frame the windows overlooking the park. Nearby, you'll find a pretty blue-and-peach room with double bed, pine floors and wicker furnishings.

Guests may use the formal living room with its tasteful dark-blue-and-cream colour scheme, or hang out in the cosy library with TV and working fireplace. If the weather's good, you'll want to settle into the verandah's colourful over-stuffed cushions on white wicker chairs, and enjoy the view.

After, stroll through the park and along the Victorian boardwalk which skirts the wide, sandy beach, and end up at the harbour and marina, a favoured spot for in-the-know sailors. Head up to the main street and take a look at the ornate Victoria Hall which houses an art gallery and Old-Bailey-style courtroom used in film shoots. Along the way, stop at a few of the interesting shops. By then, you'll probably have figured out why the Duncans (and the Globe) think so highly of this gem of a small town.

- Victoria View -

With a remarkably-preserved 19th-century building stock, Cobourg is attracting big-city folk like the Duncans to its sophisticated, small-town life-style.

103

Seasons Bed & Breakfast

Doug and Linda MacIntyre
95 King St. W.
Gananoque, ON K7G 2G2
1-888-382-7122
613-382-3822 (tel/fax)
E-mail: seasons@gananoque.com

Best time to call: anytime
Season: all year
Rates: S or D $60-115 (includes taxes)
Cards: VISA/MC/AMEX
Restrictions: children 12 and older welcome, smoking outside
Facilities: 6 bedrooms (1 twin-bedded, 2 queen, 3 king); 1 full en suite bathroom (whirlpool/shower stall), 1 en suite (shower only), 1 2-piece en suite, 2 bathrooms shared by guests; common areas for guests
Parking: off-street for 8 cars
Breakfast: full
In residence: 20 mins E of Kingston
Directions: from Hwy 401, take exit 645 (Hwy 32) and travel S to King St (Hwy 2). Turn right over bridge. Follow sharp turn. Go 1½ blocks

Tourists flock to Gananoque – it's something to do with the Thousand Islands. Kidding aside, this town is loaded with inns and B&Bs. I'll leave the inns up to someone else but my pick for the best B&B is Seasons, hosted by former Toronto residents, Doug and Linda MacIntyre. It's a fine house, indeed, with grand Victorian flourishes. Upon passing through the elaborate bevelled glass front doors, you'll find yourself in an imposing entrance hall, and to your right a large cream-carpeted "concert room" containing not much more than Doug's grand piano, which he's been known to play for appreciative guests. Adjacent, and separated by an ornate arch with ionic columns, is the guest sitting room.

There are six bedrooms here. The most recent is the Cranberry Room on the third floor with its brand new bathroom containing a whirlpool tub and shower stall. The others are on the second floor. The king-bedded Tea Rose Room is the largest with a table and chairs in the turret area. Its en suite bathroom has a shower. The cool-green-and-white Tulip Room is livened by its jaunty wallpaper border of red and yellow tulips. It has a king bed and 2-piece bathroom. Warm fawn colours are used in the queen-bedded Maple Leaf Room, sunny yellow roses in the twin bedded Briar Rose Room, and blue and white in the smaller queen-bedded Forget-Me-Not Room. These last four rooms share two large bathrooms.

Next morning you'll take breakfast in the octagon-shaped dining room. Main courses vary; perhaps crepes, souffle, or fruit-filled pancakes. After, if you're like most visitors, you'll probably head off to the docks to pick up a cruise around those famous islands. Or you can walk to the museum, historic sites, 1000 Islands Playhouse and assorted festivals. Out-of-season, Linda and Doug have put together a series of winter theme weekends. Just call and ask for their schedule.

- Season's -

My pick among the many B&Bs in this "gateway to the Thousand Islands".

105

Mulberry Grange

Helen Stephens
4852 Petworth Road
Harrowsmith, ON K0H 1V0
613-372-0411 (tel/fax)
E-mail: mulberry@istar.ca

Best time to call: anytime
Languages: French
Season: all year
Rates: S $75-90, D $116-136 (plus GST)
Cards: VISA/MC
Restrictions: children 12 and older welcome, smoking outside, enquire about guests' pets
Facilities: 3 bedrooms (1 twin, 2 queen), 3 en suite bathrooms (2 shower/tub, 1 claw foot tub plus shower), several common areas for guests; central air; phone, fax and computer available
Parking: plenty
Breakfast: full
In residence: Ollie, the boxer
Location: just north of Kingston
Directions: from Hwy 401, exit at Hwy 38. Drive 18 km to Harrowsmith. Two kms N of Harrowsmith, turn left on Petworth Rd. Drive 6 kms to sign on right

Prepare to be pampered. Mulberry Grange host Helen Stephens has thought of everything *and* has the talent to pull it off. Her interest in antiques and interior design is reflected throughout this restored 1850s limestone house. Opulent fabrics, luxury wall-coverings, down-filled sofas, fine Georgian antiques, all come together to create a most appealing B&B in the English country house tradition. Besides the drawing room for guests there's also a country sitting room with a wood-burning fireplace and exposed beams.

The three guest bedrooms upstairs all have private bathrooms with terry robes, hairdryers and high-end toiletries. I can't top Helen's own literate descriptions of the decor so here they are. Of the twin-bedded Woodlands Room she writes, "summertime blues with a handful of wild flowers scattered over patchwork quilts". The Garden Room "draws on the traditional hues of the countryside, faded roses, russets and creams create a sense of tranquility." And

of the Meadow Suite, "exuberant colour with inspiration taken from the fields and hedgerows."

Wait, there's more. Here's the list. There's the spa, with a full range of body-care treatments including facials. An in ground kidney-shaped pool. Bikes for getting around the countryside. Even a barn for your horse, if you'd like to bring it along. Helen also hosts retreats and business meetings and imports fine English antiques for sale.

Nor is there any letdown at breakfast. In fact, it's pretty elevated. Perhaps chervil frittata, brioche with poached eggs, butterscotch crepes or, for those who want it, a full English-style breakfast. As for dinner (by reservation only), Helen cooks four and five-course meals – eclectic French and English is her style – and by the time you read this, she may well have her liquor licence. Dialing yet?

Mulberry Grange

Prepare to be pampered at an English country house served up with a twist of Canadian countryside.

Collins Lake Bed & Breakfast

Cynthia and Ernie Bruns
3458 Buck Point Lane
R.R. 1, Inverary, ON K0H 1X0
613-353-1593
E-mail: clb-b@adan.kingston.net

Best time to call: anytime
Languages: German
Season: all year
Rates: S $55, D $65 (no taxes)
Restrictions: enquire about children under 7, smoking outside, no guests' pets
Facilities: 3 bedrooms (1 twin-bedded, 1 queen plus ¾ bed, 1 queen plus single); 3 bathrooms shared by guests (1 with shower and sink and 1 with toilet and sink. 1 3-piece on main floor, shower only); common areas shared with hosts; phone in kitchen
Parking: off-road for 3-4 cars
Breakfast: full
In residence: Paddy, the Lab; Hobbes & Bill, the cats
Location: 20 mins N of downtown Kingston
Directions: From Hwy 401, exit 617. Go N on Division 10.4 kms to Buck Pnt Lane. Turn right. Go 1.5 km

Driving into Collins Lake B&B, you'll find yourself on a single lane winding through a cow pasture, backed by bushland, with a ramshackle barn off to one side. Navigate down a steepish hill and "voila!" a small community of cottages reveals itself. Just along the way you'll find the B&B on a well-treed point of land surrounded by lake. The surprise is that all of this is barely 20 minutes from *downtown* Kingston.

When we arrived at Cynthia and Ernie Bruns recently-built log home, some British guests were just departing. As they left, a trail of positive comments in their wake, I was struck once again by the appeal of B&B travel -- what special memories those folks will take back with them to England. Waving good-bye to her parting guests, Cynthia greeted us and showed us around. Comforting country touches abound – primitive antiques, a cosy wood stove and fireplace, dried flowers and herbs overhead, and, everywhere, Cynthia's hand-made teddy bears. Upstairs, you'll find three nicely decorated guest bedrooms with painted wood floors. The largest has a queen-size bed and ¾ iron-and-brass bed. Its red-and-yellow colour scheme is picked up in the mats hooked by Cynthia and quilts hand-made by her mother. Another room, in white and dark blue, also has a queen size bed, plus a single. The third has twin beds with dark maroon walls lightened up with taupe and rosy reds.

For breakfast the next morning, Cynthia offers dishes like blueberry pancakes or strata cups (a baked dish with cubed bread, eggs, cheese, ham and herbs from the garden). As for Ernie, he'll probably be off early to his chemical engineering job in Kingston, but *you... You* can stick around. Row a boat. Paddle a canoe. Fish for bass and muskie. Lie about on the floating swimming dock. Or simply bask in Cynthia's perennial gardens dotted with whimsical sculptures by son, Michael. So go ahead, book a couple of nights and prepare to enjoy the Bruns' version of the Canadian cottage experience.

— Collins Lake Bed & Breakfast —

Drive just 20 minutes from downtown Kingston for a Canadian cottage experience to remember.

Limestone & Lilacs Bed & Breakfast

Monique and John Sanders
1775 Highway 38
Kingston, ON K7P 2Y7
613-545-0222
E-mail: john.sanders@sympatico.ca

Best time to call: anytime
Languages: French
Season: all year
Rates: S $55-60, D $60-85 (no taxes)
Cards: MC
Restrictions: children 10 years and older welcome, smoking on porch, no guests' pets
Facilities: 3 bedrooms (1 twin-bedded, 1 double, 1 queen); 2 bathrooms shared (both shower/tub); guest common area; central air
Parking: lots available
Breakfast: full
In residence: Benson and Emilie, the dogs; Willie, the cat (none allowed in guest areas)
Location: 15 mins NW of downtown Kingston
Directions: from Hwy 401, take exit 611. Drive N for less than 1 km. House is on left before Ducks Unlimited Conservation Area.

Limestone & Lilacs. Alliterative. Evocative. With its allusions to history and romance, just hearing the name makes you want to plan a visit to this B&B. And hosts Monique and John Sanders are not just leading you on – the historical bits are provided by their own families together with this 1820s-built limestone farmhouse. As for romance, even if you don't arrive when the air is drenched with the scent of lilacs, you'll find a gracious, beautifully decorated home that makes you feel good just being there.

From the wraparound porch you enter into the Canadiana family room with pine floors and wood-burning fireplace. Burgundy and bayberry green are the colours used to pull the room together, and one wall is exposed limestone. Here you'll find a satellite TV, a large collection of books and, discreetly off to one side, a full bathroom for guest use.

Upstairs you'll find a second bathroom and the three guest bedrooms. The Redmond Room, named after John's mom, contains her mahogany heirloom furniture. Ancestral photos trace back to John's Loyalist roots. As for Monique's roots, the Laurier Room is named after Sir Wilfred, a distant relative of hers and one of Canada's leading historical figures. Here you'll find two single four-poster beds and Laurier family pictures. A third room is named after Queen's University, alma mater to many in John's family, including himself. The slanted ceiling and deep window well provide a romantic setting for the mahogany four-poster double bed.

Next morning, you'll have breakfast in the biscuit-coloured dining room with brass chandelier overhead. Besides croissants and fresh fruit, you'll have a dish such as herb omelette or French crepes. And after, Monique brings out a freshly-baked coffee cake – could be blueberry, orange or lemon – so make sure you leave room for a slice with your last cup of coffee.

— Limestone & Lilacs Bed & Breakfast —

History and romance prevails – it's no illusion at this B&B.

Riverview

Susan Taylor
238 Rideau St.
Kingston, ON K7K 3A5
613-546-7707

Best time to call: anytime
Besides English: some French, Spanish
Season: all year
Rates: S $45, D $55-75 (no taxes)
Restrictions: well-behaved children welcome, no smoking, no guests' pets
Facilities: 3 bedrooms (2 double beds, 1 queen with pull-out); 2 bathrooms (1 en suite shower only, 1 shared with combined shower/tub); living room for guests; air conditioners in bedrooms
Parking: on site
Breakfast: full
Location: close to downtown
Directions: from Hwy 401 take Division St S. Go past 6 lights. Turn left at Railway St which curves into Rideau

Riverview B&B is as bright and cheery as host Sue Taylor herself. Young and energetic, Sue left a Toronto job with Bell Canada and moved to Kingston to start her B&B. When I arrived, she invited me to join her and another guest, a visiting prof at Queens. I enjoyed the homey combo of wine, popcorn and lively chat with the two women.

The much-improved neighbourhood is just a 15-minute walk to downtown. These 1930s worker row houses don't have quite the same cachet you'll find in tonier Kingston neighbourhoods. But you'll understand why Sue bought here when you see her view over the inner harbour of the Cataraqui River.

Inside, the house has been gutted so there isn't much left of the original, except for the hardwood floors. Upstairs, two small rooms at the front share a pretty bathroom with clawfoot tub and shower. One room has rose-and-green wallpaper and pine furnishings. The other has Wedgewood blue walls with white trim, and a mahogany spool bed. Both have ceiling fans and air conditioners.

The huge room at the back accommodates four easily. There are even twin sinks. But you'd want to know each other *very* well – the shower is actually "in-suite," only partly hidden behind a screen. (The toilet *is* behind a closed door.) Golds and rust suit the colonial styling of the queen-size cannonball bed and double sofa bed. This room also has an air conditioner in the summer.

The sun was streaming into the dining room when I came down for breakfast. It's set up buffet-style and includes bacon and eggs. And with Sue's bright personality I couldn't have had a sunnier start to my day. Unless I'd had my eggs sunny-side-up.

- Riverview -

Here you'll find a friendly, energetic host and a bright and cheery B&B.

113

Secret Garden Bed & Breakfast

Maryanne and John Baker
73 Sydenham St.
Kingston, ON K7L 3H3
613-531-9884
E-mail:
baker@the-secret-garden.com

Best time to call: 10 AM to 10 PM
Season: all year
Rates: S or D $75-120 (plus taxes)
Cards: VISA/AMEX/DINERS/ENROUTE
Restrictions: children 10 and older welcome, smoking outside, no guests' pets
Facilities: 4 bedrooms (2 double, 1 queen, 1 king); 4 en suite bathrooms (1 double Jacuzzi with hand-held shower, 3 shower/tub); living room for guests; central air
Parking: off-street for 3 cars
Breakfast: full
In residence: Muffin, the cat; 2 20-something offspring
Location: downtown Kingston
Directions: from Toronto, take Hwy 401 exit 615 (Sir John A. MacDonald) and go 5 stop lights to Johnson St. Turn left. Go 2-3 km to Sydenham St. Turn right.

It won't be a secret for long. The Secret Garden B&B is smack dab in the middle of downtown Kingston: two minutes to the waterfront, two minutes to downtown, two minutes to Queen's University. And, my dear, it's to die for.

First off, host Maryanne Baker has all the right qualities – warm, accommodating and gracious. *And* she knows how to make a great cup of tea. This is important. Hear ye! Hear ye! All hosts who serve tea American-style with bag out. *Ask* us if we'd like it made the traditional *Canadian* way. I really got fed up with tea that tasted like dishwater this past research phase. End of rant.

The accommodations here are first-rate and the decor is an imaginative take on traditional. It starts outside with several attractive seating areas for guests: two wicker-furnished porches, plus a private flower-filled courtyard with fountain. Inside, there's a gracious guest living room with ornate fireplace and, upstairs, four large bedrooms all with private bath. There's lots of mahogany and oriental carpets, and each has its own comfortable sitting area. Victoria Rose has a plantation-style four-poster queen-size bed and a two-person Jacuzzi right in the room. Theresa's Room has a king-size four-poster bed with canopy. Angels' Watch has a peaches-and-cream decor with an antique four-poster double pineapple bed from Bath, Maine. And the Secret Garden Room has another pineapple bed, and features most of Agatha Christie's novels. It has a private balcony overlooking the garden below.

Next morning, your breakfast could very well be something like fruit with vanilla-yogurt dressing, vegetable-and-Cheddar quiche and peach-raspberry coffee cake. You'll have it either in the oak-panelled dining room with stained glass windows, the screened side porch or outside in the courtyard if the weather co-operates. And soon, I guarantee it, you'll be telling secrets, too.

the Secret Garden

This B&B won't be a secret for long.

Jackson's Falls Schoolhouse B&B

Pete and Nancy Fleck
R.R. 2, County Rd. 17
Milford, ON K0K 2P0
613-476-8576 (phone or FAX)

Best time to call: anytime
Besides English: French
Season: all year
Rates: S or D $55-70 (no taxes)
Restrictions: children over 10 welcome, smoking in common area if other guests approve, no guests' pets
Facilities: 6 bedrooms (1 queen, 1 queen and single, 2 double, 2 double and single); 2 en suite bathrooms (combined shower/tub); 2 en suite bathrooms (sink & toilet only) share room with combined shower/tub; 2 rooms share bathroom with combined shower/tub; school-room common area for guests; FAX
Parking: plenty on site
Breakfast: full
In residence: Jackson and Freyja, springer spaniels; and Kit E. Cat
Location: south of Hwy 401 at Belleville, 2½ hours east of Toronto, 3½ from Montreal
Directions: 2 km east of Milford on County Rd 17

Energetic forties-something couple quits the Toronto ad-game. Take themselves off to "the County". And start a B&B. Strike a chord? Probably because it's the dream of hundreds, fulfilled by the very few. But Pete and Nancy Fleck did it. Got away to all that bucolic countryside. The slower pace. They even have a greenhouse for heaven's sake!

After moving to the County (as Prince Edward County is known) in 1988, the Flecks restored this 1870s-built one-room schoolhouse and added a topsy-like addition with four B&B guest rooms. One, the Annan Room has a two-person Jacuzzi tub right in the room – the rest of the bathroom's behind closed doors. This room has a double bed with a fan pattern quilt. Another, the Tottenham Room, has a double bed and an antique fainting couch facing the fireplace. There's a full bathroom en suite. Besides two more rooms in the addition, you'll find a further two rooms above the workshop nearby. These last two share a bathroom *plus* a small deck overlooking the river.

The 700-square-foot "schoolroom" is where guests gather. The blackboards, light fixtures, and woodstove were there before. But now there's also a homelike lounge and large dining area with three tables. Which brings us to dinner. The Flecks will do meals for $15 per person. Their specialty is rack of lamb but they'll do other things as well. What I like is that B&B guests bring their own wine.

Next morning you'll have the usual assortment of muffins, fruit, cereal, and eggs any way you like. After that, it's farewell to the County and back to big-city life. Unless it's, "Honey, let's check out that For Sale sign we saw down the road."

116

-Jackson's Falls Schoolhouse B&B-

Leave the rat race behind and hie yourself off to "the County" – just like the hosts of this B&B.

The Poplars

Jean Whitney
R.R. 2
Picton, ON K0K 2T0
613-476-3513

Best time to call: anytime
Season: all year
Rates: S $40, D $45-60 (no taxes)
Restrictions: no smoking, no guests' pets
Facilities: 4 bedrooms (2 twin-bedded, 1 queen, 1 double); 1 private bathroom (combined shower/tub); 1 bathroom shared only by guests (combined shower/tub); living room and family room for guests; central air; 2 barbecues available
Parking: on site
Breakfast: full
Location: a good 2-hour drive east of Toronto; about 18 kms north of the town of Picton
Directions: take exit 566 (Hwy 49) from Hwy 401. Drive south 10 kms. Turn right on Northport Rd. Go 1 km to The Poplars

The Poplars is a good place for an overnight stay if you're travelling along the 401, or sailing around the Bay of Quinte. Just five minutes off the highway, it's a huge house, built around 1900, right on the bay. Three acres of lawn slope down to a dock, with space for four boats.

Though built at the turn of the century, this house doesn't feel old inside. That's because it's more of a renovation than a restoration, with contemporary furnishings. The guest bedrooms, all on the second floor, are broadloomed and pleasantly coordinated in pretty colours with comfortable seating.

We stayed in the Green Room, which has extra-long twin beds with fabric-upholstered headboards. There's also a room with a double bed, and one with twin beds that's smaller. If you want an en suite bathroom, the peach-and-blue queen-bedded room has one.

Host Jean Whitney will *never* be accused of stinting on breakfast. It can only be called substantial. You get eggs and bacon *and* ham *and* sausage *and* fried mushrooms *and* homefries. The food just keeps coming. And she'll cook your eggs any way you want 'em. We had our breakfast in the dining room, but in warmer weather, you'll probably take it on the deck overlooking the bay.

— The Poplars —

The Poplars is a good place for an overnight stay if you're travelling along the 401. Or if you're sailing around the Bay of Quinte – there's dock space for four boats.

119

Timm's Grandview Manor

Rikki and Dieter Timm
R.R. 2
Picton, ON K0K 2T0
613-476-8875 (fax 476-7272)

Best time to call: anytime
Languages: German
Season: all year
Rates: S or D $70-120 (no taxes)
enquire about off-season rates
Restrictions: children over 12
welcome, smoking outside, no
guests' pets
Facilities: 3 bedrooms (2 twin-
bedded, 1 double); 3 en suite
bathrooms (all with shower/tub; 1
of the en suites is shared) main
floor living room and upper hall
alcove for guests; ceiling fans;
mobile phone; fax available at cost
Parking: off-street for many cars
Breakfast: full
Location: about 2 hrs and 20 mins
from Toronto; 30 mins south of
Belleville
Directions: from Hwy 401, take
exit 566 (Hwy 49) and drive south
about 26 kms to the first driveway
before Edgecliffe Road

Timm's Grandview Manor has to be one of
the most interesting homes in this book.
Appearing a hundred years older than it
actually is, it was built in the 1930s by a
wealthy ex-New Yorker. When you arrive
you'll be welcomed by hosts Rikki and
Dieter Timm in the magnificent entrance
hall with curving staircase. A tour of
downstairs takes you through the unique
panelled gallery room and, off to one side,
you'll find the sunken living room with
crystal chandeliers and several sitting areas
for guests.

Upstairs, you'll find yourself in a spacious hall with a sitting alcove. Of the three
guest bedrooms, the biggest is the
Grandview, aptly-named for its view over
the Timms' three-and-a-half acres of lawn
and gardens sloping down to their dock on
Picton Bay. The room's Asian-theme decor
is enhanced by soft creams and greens, with
sharp hits of tangerine. Two extra-long
double beds don't even begin to crowd the
space. And besides the private bathroom
and large sitting area, there's a full-size
balcony for taking in the panoramic view.
You may even be enticed to join fellow guests
down below in a game of croquet or badminton.

The South Garden View Room has taupe
walls and a continental theme. Its extra-long
twin beds have Persian-rug headboards, plus
there's a sitting area and large four-piece
bath. The twin-bedded North Garden View
Room has a shared bathroom, conveniently
accessed from within your room (others
access this bathroom through a second door).

Next morning, Rikki accommodates
breakfast requests, but if they're fully
booked, she'll make an executive decision
about the main course; coming up with
something like a cheese-vegetable strata with
homemade scones, or buttermilk pancakes
with strawberry-orange-lemon sauce. She'll
also do imaginative dinners for groups of
four or more if they're arranged in advance –
often around such exotic themes as Thai or
Indian.

120

Timm's Grandview Manor

The view doesn't get any grander than this.

Butternut Inn Bed & Breakfast

Bob and Bonnie Harrison
36 North St
Port Hope, ON L1A 1T8
905-885-4318 (fax 885-5464)
E-mail: info@butternutinn.com

Best time to call: before 10 AM or after 3 PM
Season: all year
Rates: S $60-70, D $70-95 (plus taxes)
Cards: VISA/MC
Restrictions: children over 13 welcome, smoking outside, no guests' pets
Facilities: 4 bedrooms (4 queen); 4 bathrooms; 3 en suite (1 shower/ tub, 2 shower only), 1 private-use (shower/whirlpool tub); living room, and solarium for guests; portable phone
Parking: off-street for 4 cars
Breakfast: full
In residence: Peaches and Wolfgang, the cats
Location: 1 hour E of Toronto
Directions: from Hwy 401, take exit 461. Follow Hwy 2 S. Turn left onto Ridout St. Turn left onto Pine. Go 2 blocks to North St. Turn right

Tucked away off Port Hope's main street, but close to all the antique and specialty shops, you'll find the Butternut Inn B&B and its amiable hosts, Bob and Bonnie Harrison. It starts with the attractive gardens – in the park-like grounds out back you'll find a vast range of shrubs and perennials.

Inside, there's a comfortable living room for guests and, through the dining room, a solarium with wood stove overlooking the back gardens. Upstairs, you'll find four appealing guest bedrooms, all with top-quality mattresses on queen-size beds covered with silk quilts in summer and down duvets in cooler weather. You'll also appreciate the bathroom dispensers with shampoo, shower gel and conditioner.

The largest room is the "chintzy" Kew Gardens, with its four-poster bed, and a small sofa which makes into a single bed. Influences of the French countryside can be found in the yellow-and-blue Avignon Room. The Italian Garden Room is deco-rated in rose, green and gold and overlooks the back gardens. Farini's Studio has deep plum walls and African artifacts – it's a real original, just like the infamous Port Hope daredevil it's named after. You'll find its private bathroom just down the hall.

Bonnie's an accomplished cook, so her breakfasts always garner rave reviews. Here's a sample menu. Fresh fruit compote with ginger-yogurt sauce, Farini's frittata (a baked omelette of ham, apples and onions), home fries, and herbed tomatoes. And to top it off, cinnamon-swirl biscuits. Bonnie's love of cooking has led the Harrisons into a popular venture – they run "Gourmet Getaway Weekends" a couple of times a month. Bonnie does Friday night dinner and gregarious chef-instructor, Lynne Timermanis, gives a cooking lesson Saturday evening, after which all sit down to enjoy the spoils. Lots of fun and laughter and a great stress-buster. For current dates and prices contact the Harrisons by phone or e-mail.

- Butternut Inn B&B -

Come and be spoiled by engaging hosts, appealing rooms and extra-special breakfasts.

Hillcrest

Ruth Beaucage
175 Dorset St. W.
Port Hope, ON L1A 1G4
905-885-7367
905-885-8167 (fax)

Best time to call: 9 AM to 5 PM
Besides English: German
Season: all year
Rates: S $95-105, D $110-120
(plus PST & GST)
Cards: VISA/MC
Restrictions: no children under
14, no smoking, no guests' pets
Facilities: 5 bedrooms (1 twin-
bedded, 3 queen, 1 king), 2 with
private balconies; all with private
bath (3 with combined shower/
tub, 1 with tub, 1 with Jacuzzi);
living room for guests; sauna and
in-ground pool
Parking: plenty on site
Breakfast: continental
In residence: Beau, the standard
poodle
Location: 1 hour east of Toronto
Directions: exit Hwy 401 at Hwy
2. At first light in Port Hope turn
left. Go 1 block. Turn right on
Bramley, which turns into Dorset

When you drive through the gates of
Hillcrest, you'll wonder if you've arrived at
a mansion straight out of *Gone with the
Wind*. It's not surprising – the classical
decorative style of Hillcrest was developed
in the 19th century by the Ecole des Beaux
Arts in Paris, and often found in southern
plantations. Over the past several years,
host Ruth Beaucage has applied her
unquenchable energy to its restoration.

Once you've stopped gaping in wonder
at the grounds, inside, you'll find bright,
spacious, high-ceilinged rooms and decor
reflecting Ruth's distinctive style. Through
an archway to your right as you enter, is
the formal living room with walls covered
in yellow moire. Its elegant furnishings are
grouped around a fireplace, with a grand
piano in one corner.

Upstairs, choosing a favourite room is
difficult because there's something to like
about every one. Three of the five rooms
even have fireplaces. Herewith, a sampling
of two. The pink-and-burgundy Master

Bedroom features a Jacuzzi tub in its
adjoining bathroom. The bedroom has a
grey marble fireplace, and from its walkout
balcony you can look out over the gardens
and ravine to Lake Ontario.

Another is the romantic Flower Room
with cream-coloured canopy bed. The
Victorian-inspired wallpaper has a bold
floral design in gold and cream with
touches of blue and green. Two loveseats
and other furnishings are done in neutral
colours. Its en suite bathroom has a contemporary tub and shower.

Breakfast is served in the spacious
glassed-in sun room with fireplace which
looks south over the lake. It's very much in
the continental European mode; starting
with a fruit cup, followed by a cheese tray
along with pastries and Danish.

And be sure to ask Ruth about her spa
facilities when you book ...perhaps a
massage or facial will be just what you
need.

- Hillcrest -

You'll feel like you've arrived at Gone With the Wind's Tara when you drive through the gates of Hillcrest. It's designed in the same beaux arts style as southern colonial mansions.

125

The Ganders

Jeremy and Carol Gander
22 Beach Street, P.O. Box 175
Wellington, ON K0K 3L0
613-399-1987 (tel/fax)
E-mail: jcgander@connect.reach.net

Best time to call: anytime
Season: all year
Rates: S $45-60, D $65-80 (no taxes)
Cards: VISA
Restrictions: children 6 and older welcome, smoking outside, enquire about guests' pets
Facilities: 3 queen bedrooms with en suite bathrooms (1 shower/whirlpool tub, 2 2-pce), 1 shared bathroom shower/tub only; library and parlour for guests; central air; phone in kitchen
Parking: off-street for 3 cars
Breakfast: full
In residence: Schatze, the spaniel
Location: on Lake Ontario, 2½ hrs E of Toronto
Directions: Wellington is on Hwy 33 in Prince Edward County. Beach Street runs south from the main street, near the water tower at east end of town

They've taken to it like ducks to water. The Ganders to B&B on the water, that is. Jeremy and Carol Gander are offering a fine B&B right on Lake Ontario, and they're providing all the amenities we fussy guests like to have. A friendly welcome, attractive accommodations with extras like hairdryers and bathrobes, a fruit-and-cookie plate in your room, and something special for breakfast. The Ganders built this garrison-style house in 1994 on a large lakefront property, *especially* to do B&B. So there was no need to reconfigure an old house to offer privacy. They were able to build it right in.

Though right in the village of Wellington, the Ganders' property is somewhat secluded situated as it is amongst groves of mature trees and surrounded by perennial gardens designed to complement the landscape's natural beauty. Take a path down to the pebble beach and you can walk along the shore to the public beach a stone's throw away.

Inside, the three guest bedrooms are upstairs. The largest is the rich red-and-gold Master Suite with a four-poster queen-size bed and Persian rug. Its spacious bathroom has two sinks, a shower stall and large Jacuzzi bath. The other two rooms have en suite two-piece bathrooms and they share a separate room with tub and shower. The Green Room has a writing desk and tub chair and The Blue Room's large window overlooks the gardens and lakeshore. Both have queen-size beds.

Next morning, you'll have breakfast in the dining room. Carol cooks and Jeremy does the serving. When I was there, Carol made a crepe with quiche filling, but she has quite a repetoire, including a dish I'd like the next time: rice-flour cottage-cheese pancakes with fresh fruit. After, take your last cup of coffee out to the patio and plan your day – you're in the heart of bucolic Prince Edward County here, so intriguing possibilities await.

- The Ganders -

A house built especially for B&B in a secluded garden setting on Lake Ontario.

Capricorn Capers

Les and Wendy Wert
5480 SDG Road 19
Williamstown, ON K0C 2J0
613-347-3098
E-mail: capricorn@cnwl.igs.net

Best time to call: anytime
Season: all year
Rates: S $35, D $60 (no taxes)
Restrictions: no smoking, no guests' pets
Facilities: 3 bedrooms (1 twin-bedded, 1 queen, 1 king); 3 en suite bathrooms (shower/tub), study and living room for guests; telephone in twin room and office; computer and fax available (with calling card)
Parking: off-street for 6 cars
Breakfast: full
In residence: Pepper, the schnauzer
Location: 1½ hrs SE of Ottawa; 1 hr W of Montreal
Directions: from Hwy 401, exit 814 at Lancaster. Take Hwy 34 N to Pine St. (SDG Rd 17). Turn left on Pine and drive 7 km to Williamstown. At 4-way stop, turn right onto Johnson Rd (SDG Rd 19). Drive 1.8 km to second house on left

A youngster compared to most other homes in this book, Capricorn Capers is a mere quarter-century old. But it *is* situated in one of the most historical sections of Ontario so if you want antiquity, you'll find it all around – we discovered a church in Williamstown dated 1787. And just 40 minutes away you'll find Upper Canada Village.

Hosts Wendy and Les Wert chose this house for their B&B for a number of reasons. First, the views over ponds and meadows appealed immensely. Second, the accommodations were spacious and they could offer private bathrooms with all rooms. And third, they thought Williamstown made a great overnight stop for folks travelling Highway 401 between Montreal (an hour away) and points west.

When you arrive, Wendy welcomes you in the large cream-carpeted foyer. Adjoining it you'll see the study where guests usually gather. With a fireplace and chintz-covered furnishings, it's a cosy spot for conversation or curling up with a good book. There's also a TV, VCR and CD player. Upstairs, the guest bedrooms are available year-round. They're nicely decorated and look out in various directions over the countryside.

But if you're there between May and October, here's a tip – I suspect you'll be *really* happy with the king-bedded main-floor Master Suite with walkout to an attractive patio with small pond. Its recently-renovated bathroom is on the luxe side and has a Jacuzzi tub. We missed getting it because we were last-minute drop-ins – we liked our room very much, but once we'd seen Paree... Reservations are a must!

Breakfast is usually an egg dish of some sort. We had bacon and eggs, but you may be offered pancakes or French toast. After, why not take a hike around the property, or do what a lot of visitors do in this part of the Province, go visit some old graveyards – they're sure to be *really* old.

- Capricorn Capers -

Reservations are a must for the main floor Master Suite with walkout to pond and patio.

129

Caron House (1837)

Mary and Michael Caron
South Branch Rd.
P.O. Box 143
Williamstown, ON K0C 2J0
613-347-7338

Best time to call: anytime
Besides English: French
Season: all year
Rates: S $40, D $50
(no taxes)
Restrictions: children over 14 welcome, no smoking, no guests' pets
Facilities: 2 bedrooms (2 double); 1 bathroom shared only by guests (tub only); den and parlour with fireplaces, garden, verandah and gazebo for guests to enjoy
Parking: in lane, next to green carriage shed
Breakfast: full
In residence: Inky, the toy poodle
Location: near Quebec border. One-hour drive west of Montreal or southeast of Ottawa
Directions: across from St. Mary's Church in Williamstown

A soft snow drifted down as I drove up to Caron House one evening. To my surprise each window had a candle in it. This attention to nice touches is what makes Caron House so special. Mary has an unerring sense of design, colour and what works. Wallpapers from New York, Laura Ashley fabrics and an outstanding selection of antiques all combine beautifully.

Mary grew up in Williamstown, a village that's now a couple of centuries old. As a little girl she would visit the woman who lived in the house and sit by the fire and dream that it was her own. Years later her dream came true. The Carons bought this Georgian house which remains structurally unchanged from when it was built in 1837. The parlours still have their tin ceilings and the windows, their original inside shutters.

I was the only guest so I had my choice of bedrooms. Hard decision, this. Both have Laura Ashley wallpapers with hooked scatter rugs on painted pine floors. I could just as easily have gone for the yellow room, but settled on the pink-and-white one with iron double bed covered with antique linens and handmade quilts. I was charmed to know that this room had once combined with the large bathroom next door to make a ballroom. People arrived by carriage on Saturday nights for dances and music-making.

You'll find treats for the eye in every nook and cranny. And this is a place where, when they say "gourmet" it's not just an ad, they mean it. Served by candlelight, my breakfast was pineapple banana frappé, and a special French toast with almonds and honey-orange sauce served on Royal Doulton china and Waterford crystal, while a Strauss waltz played in the background.

After breakfast, I have no doubt you'll want to pause awhile in the Caron's garden if you're there during summer. They've lavished the same attention on it as on the rest of the place.

— Caron House —

One of the most beautifully restored B&B's in the province – painstaking attention to detail, exquisite taste and gourmet breakfasts make it extra special.

131

Menzies House 1853

Pat and Frank Vetter
80 Queen Street
Almonte, ON K0A 1A0
613-256-2055

Best time to call: morning or evening
Season: all year
Rates: S $60, D $70 (no taxes)
Restrictions: smoking in gazebo only, children over 10 welcome, no guests' pets
Facilities: 2 guest rooms (1 twin-bedded, 1 king); 1 bathroom shared by guests (shower/tub); guests may also use library, living room, gazebo and pool; air conditioning in bedrooms
Parking: off-street for 2 cars
Breakfast: full
Location: 33 km from Ottawa
Directions: from Ottawa via Hwys 417 and 49, turn left at first stop light (Queen St), drive to first house on right before bridge. From Toronto via Hwy 7 and 29, take first exit into Almonte. Drive along Perth & Bridge streets. Go through stop light and over bridge to first house on left

"Come as a guest and leave as a friend." That's the motto of Menzies House hosts Pat and Frank Vetter and they couldn't have lived up to it better. The genuine welcome, the tea in the library provided by Frank, and the gracious comfortable look of the place. It all works together to create a B&B you want to return to again and again, just as with good friends. And like good friends, if you rely on public transport, Pat and Frank will even arrange to pick you up in Ottawa.

The 1853-built house itself is Anglo-Norman in design, one more commonly found in Quebec. In the 1860s, the lower level was a general store. Now though, the commerce is limited to the two B&B rooms which share a large bathroom on the second floor. A room with a king-size bed overlooks the river and is adjacent to the bathroom. Both it and the bathroom are decorated with Waverley prints, sewn by Pat. The twin-bedded room, along the hall, has Sanderson fabrics and is on the street-side. On the main level guests are welcome to use the living room with fireplace, and the library which has a TV and VCR.

There's much to enjoy outside at Menzies House as well; what with a pool and gazebo, 250 feet of gardens and lawn sloping down to the river, and a canoe you can borrow for a paddle. A bit further afield, all within walking distance, are several good-to-excellent restaurants.

Next morning you'll have breakfast in the formal dining room – mine was by candlelight. The breakfast main dish might be smoked salmon crepes accompanied by Scotch scones. I was a last-minute, out-of-season drop-in and even then Pat came up with a delicious breakfast for one. (Much appreciated, I might add. I often run into a ho-hum breakfast in this situation.) After, Pat invited me into the kitchen where I was intrigued by some framed recipes on the wall. Turns out they were handwritten by three generations of Pat's family. To me they typify the warmth of this home.

— Menzies House —

"Come as a guest and leave as a friend."

133

Old Burnside

Marilyn and Howard Campbell
218 Hamilton Street
P.O. Box 1782
Almonte/Mississippi Mills, ON
K0A 1A0
613-256-2066 (fax 256-2023)

Best time to call: before 10 PM
Languages: German, French, Spanish
Season: all year
Rates: S $60-70, D $65-75 (no taxes)
Restrictions: enquire about children, smoking in garden, enquire about guests' pets
Facilities: 3 bedrooms (1 queen, 1 twin-bedded, 1 double); 1 en suite bathroom (shower/tub); 1 either shared or en suite on third floor with shower/separate tub; living room for guests; mobile phone; fax available at cost
Parking: off-street for 5-8 cars
Breakfast: full
Location: 45 mins W of Ottawa on NW edge of Almonte
Directions: obtain when booking

This castle-like Georgian home sits grandly on the banks of the fast-flowing Mississipi River with a 25-foot waterfall nearby. Having retired, hosts Howard and Marilyn Campbell decided to share their impressive home with B&B travellers. When we arrived we were warmly welcomed and, before dinner, we sat with Howard and Marilyn in their massive living room and chatted about the interesting furnishings, many discovered locally or collected in their travels.

Three B&B rooms are available on the second and third floors, and all show evidence of Marilyn's eclectic decorating style. On the second floor you'll find the grandly-proportioned Tait McKenzie Suite which has a queen-size bed, en suite bathroom and overlooks the gardens and waterfall. Up to the third floor for the other two. The Naismith Room, named for the local who invented basketball, has twin beds and deep window wells offering views in two directions. The James Wylie Aerie, named for Old Burnside's builder, is a corner room done in blue and white with a queen-size bed. These two share a bathroom, but it can be private if requested.

At breakfast the next morning, the castle ambiance was reinforced when we sat ourselves down in the dining room, complete with heavy wood furniture and an 11-foot stone hearth, host to an ancient iron crane used originally to hoist the cooking pots. As for breakfast – what delights awaited. Along with juice and fresh fruit we had an asparagus and goat cheese quiche followed by a cranberry walnut tart. *Your* breakfast might be prosciutto, mushroom and leek strata followed by caramelized lemon pie. Whew! Marilyn *can* accommodate requests for low-cholesterol breakfasts, if done so in advance. Otherwise, she has a policy of being "unabashadly caloric". My kind of gal.

-Old Burnside Bed & Breakfast-

Warm and gracious hosts in a castle-like setting plus an "unabashedly caloric" breakfast.

135

Inglenook Bed & Breakfast

Barbara and David Newing
P.O. Box 234
Barry's Bay, ON K0J 1B0
613-756-0727

Best time to call: anytime
Season: all year
Rates: S $40, D $55 (no taxes)
Restrictions: enquire about children, smoking outside, no guests' pets
Facilities: 2 bedrooms (1 twin-bedded, 1 queen); 1 bathroom shared by guests only (shower/tub), common area for guests; central air; mobile telephone
Parking: plenty off-road
Breakfast: full
Location: 2½ hrs W of Ottawa; 1 hr E of Algonquin Park
Directions: from Barry's Bay Hospital, drive 1½ kms S. Turn left onto Kartuzi Rd. Drive 0.7 km and turn right, staying on Kartuzi Rd. Go 5.2 km to B&B

Inglenook B&B is a Canadian Shield gem nestled on the shores of Kamaniskeg Lake just an hour's drive from the east entrance to Algonquin Park. Hosts Barbara and David Newing built Inglenook in 1971 as a summer cottage for their young family. With children grown, they renovated, winterized and created a retreat for their retirement. Then, with a separate area that could be completely given over to guests, the Newings decided to open their home to B&B.

As you drive in, the first thing you'll notice are the extensive perennial beds in and around the rocks and outcroppings. Not surprisingly, Barbara's passion is gardening. After greeting you, she'll lead you down a gentle slope to the home's lower level, entered through French doors set into a 12-foot high wall of windows. You'll find yourself in a large room with fireplace and comfortable furnishings. Along the hall, are two smallish bedrooms, with a shared bathroom at the end. All is nicely decorated, spotlessly clean and both bedrooms have windows overlooking the lake. I was there in Fall, and my timing was perfect; the view from those windows was glorious – sparkling water, clumps of birch trees, and the distant shore a blaze of colour.

The next morning, Barbara and David do breakfast upstairs in their dining nook with windows all round, or out on the deck, so you can inhale the view. And they'll cook a breakfast to satisfy your whims. There's always several cereals, seasonal fresh fruit and then it's your choice. Bacon and eggs? Ham and eggs? An omelette? Pancakes with local maple syrup? And the eggs will be any way you want them, cooked to order.

After, you may want to go for a hike or take a swim off the dock before heading off to the many local attractions. The Newings are a gold-mine of information –the only difficulty will be in the choosing.

Inglenook Bed & Breakfast

A gem of a B&B set in the
Canadian Shield.

brilliant.
28.5.98

Hudson House

Janet McGinnis and
David Somppi
7 Lorne St.
Carleton Place, ON K7C 2J9
613-257-8547

Best time to call: mornings and late afternoon
Season: all year
Rates: S $45, D $50 (no taxes)
Restrictions: no smoking, no guests' pets
Facilities: 3 bedrooms; 2 bathrooms shared only by guests (1 with tub, 1 with shower); air-conditioned second-floor guest sitting room
Parking: on site
Breakfast: full
In residence: school-age sons, Brendon & Devin
Location: a 40-minute drive southwest of Ottawa
Directions: follow Lake Ave east from traffic lights at foot of Bridge St. After railway crossing, Lorne is 6th street on left

Hudson House is located on a quiet, tree-lined street in Carleton Place. David's an engineer with Northern Telecom and Janet, whose profession is town-planner, stays at home with their two sons and runs the B&B. They decided to get into the B&B game because they'd stayed at many themselves, and enjoyed the "home-away-from-home" atmosphere.

Upstairs, there are three serene-looking bedrooms and a guest sitting room with bright contemporary furniture and lots of plants. It comes with a colour TV and everything you need for making tea or coffee. The Pink Room, my favourite, has a walnut bedroom suite with double bed. The drapes are cream and rose with a bedspread in matching fabric. There's also a single bed in this room. The Green Room has a mahogany bedroom suite with a double bed and two easy chairs. The comforter matches the drapes which are white with a soft green floral pattern. The third room has a double bed, with a large-print floral wallpaper in blue and rose, and an heirloom spread with rose pillows.

After breakfast in the dining room, with its crystal chandelier and antique dining room suite, you can explore Lanark County. Drive to Mississippi Lake in 15 minutes, and to the Rideau Lakes in less than an hour. Or stick around Carleton Place. Swimming, fishing, boating and shopping are within walking distance of your "home-away-from-home."

– Hudson House –

Hosts, David and Janet, have enjoyed the "home-away-from-home" feel of B&B travel themselves, and strive to provide the same thing for their guests.

Denaut Mansion Country Inn

Deborah and David Peets
5 Mathew Street
Delta, ON K0E 1G0
613-928-2588 (phone/fax)

Best time to call: anytime
Season: all year (minimum two nights on summer and long weekends)
Rates: S $98-115, D $110-135 (plus taxes)
Cards: VISA/MC
Restrictions: children in apartment only, no smoking, no guests' pets
Facilities: 6 bedrooms (incl 2 in apt) 1 twin-bedded, 2 double, 3 queen; 1 powder room, 5 en suite bathrooms (1 with shower/tub, 4 with shower only); living room, bar, enclosed verandah for guests; central air; phone & fax available
Parking: off-street for 7 cars
Breakfast: extended continental
In residence: Puss, the cat
Location: 40 mins NE of Kingston
Directions: from Hwy 401 go north on Hwy 15. Turn E on Rd 33. Turn W on Rd 42 to Delta. Mathew St is on right

From the moment you enter the richly-hued foyer of Denaut Mansion Country Inn with its oriental rug and Georgian chaise, you know you're in for something special. The decor is contemporary, complementing the truly great bones of this Norman-styled stone house. Fine antiques meld ever-so-subtly with the uniquely crafted modern furnishings. Soothing neutral tones artfully combine with vibrant colours, including original works of art. Upstairs, all guest rooms are similarly appointed. *Very* tasteful. And *very* nineties. There is also a two-bedroom cottage-like apartment available.

The two behind this enticing venture are David and Deborah Peets who left Toronto financial jobs behind to realize their dream in Delta. Their idea is to provide a country house getaway, with dinner, wine and other amenities in luxurious surroundings. Self-taught cook, Deborah offers delectable three-course meals for $35 a person. And there *is* a liquor license; a list of wines to please even the oenophile range from $23-46. These prices cover tax and there is no service charge.

Breakfast is substantial continental and includes granola and local apple cider, both organic, along with homemade croissants, breads and preserves. A nice touch – a morning cappuccino if you so desire.

Now, what to do at a country house. Well, you *could* just sit back and relax, read a bit, and laze around the heated in ground pool. Or you could choose a more active regime. Keen cyclists themselves, the Peets have mapped out ten looped routes – just bring your own bikes. You could take out a canoe, hike in the nearby Provincial Parks or go antiquing. In winter, walking and cross-country skiing are naturals. Or how about digging out those long-neglected skates and going for a spin, either on Delta's own outdoor rink, or a few minutes away on a cleared section of the Rideau Canal.

Denaut Mansion Country Inn

A luxurious country house for your delectation. Prepare to be pampered.

141

Tranquility Bed & Breakfast

Maureen and Bruce Carson
1364 3rd Line Rd, R.R. #2
Lakefield, ON K0L 2H0
705-652-1639
E-mail: tranquil@oncomdis.on.ca

Best time to call: anytime
Season: all year
Rates: S $55, D $70 (plus GST)
Restrictions: smoking on porch only, no guests' pets
Facilities: 3 rooms (1 twin-bedded, 1 double, 1 queen); 2 baths shared (1 shower, 1 shower/tub), 1 2-piece shared; guest common areas; air conditioning; phone, fax & computer available
Breakfast: full
In residence: Amanda & Madison, the collies; and 5 cats
Location: ½ hour E of Peterboro
Directions: from Hwy 401, exit Hwy 115 N to Hwy 7. Turn right. Go to Rd 134. Turn left. Go to Road 4. Follow Road 4 right through Warsaw. Turn left at gas station (follow Warsaw Caves signs) and drive to B&B sign. Turn right to end of road. Go left to first house over bridge

Off the beaten track, surrounded by trees, and set on the winding banks of the Indian River, this B&B is aptly named. Tranquility B&B hosts Maureen and Bruce Carson moved from Toronto to this 1830s Georgian stone house with log addition, attracted by the idyllic location. Bruce still commutes to his financial advisor job in Toronto and Maureen runs the B&B and a small antique shop on the premises.

The B&B quarters are in the stone house. There's an antique-filled sitting room on the main floor and upstairs three bedrooms for guests. All have down-filled duvets, good reading lights and are decorated with silk flowers and porcelain dolls. A welcome touch – you'll also find ice water and chocolates. One room has a queen-size canopy bed and balloon curtains in shades of pink and blue. Another has an iron-and-brass double bed and is decorated in white eyelet with mauve and turquoise accents in the balloon curtains and rag rugs. It has a door directly into a large shared bathroom – other guests have access from the hall. The twin-bedded room is done in mint green and pink with Jessica McClintok sheets and towels.

Next morning the gregarious Maureen serves breakfast from her open kitchen in the log addition. Lots of juice, fruit and baked goodies plus something like blueberry-cinnamon pancakes, French toast or Maureen's "very special scrambled eggs". After, you might want to set a spell on the verandah, wander through the two miles of mowed trails, or take a canoe out for a quiet paddle down the river. If you can stir yourself from this tranquil haven, you could always go spelunking in the Warsaw caves just one minute away by car.

Winter brings its pleasures, too. Curl up with a good book by the fireplace or plan to do some cross-county skiing. Also, if it's arranged in advance, Maureen will do dinners. Prices range from $15 to $25 for a three-course meal.

Tranquility Bed & Breakfast

Bucolic countryside, a winding river – it's all so tranquil.

143

Millisle B&B

Derry and Kathy Thompson
P.O. Box 341
205 Mill St.
Merrickville, ON K0G 1N0
613-269-3627

Best time to call: anytime
Season: all year
Rates: S $58, D $68 (plus PST & GST)
Cards: VISA/MC/AMEX
Restrictions: not suitable for children; smoking on verandah only; no guests' pets
Facilities: 5 bedrooms (1 twin-bedded, 3 queen, 1 king); 5 private bathrooms; parlour and games/TV room for guests; central air;
Parking: plenty on site
Breakfast: full
Location: less than a 1-hour drive south-west of Ottawa or a half hour north of Hwy 401. B&B is a 2-minute walk from downtown
Directions: on the main road through town, next to the bridge

Not only does this lavish 1850s Victorian house have much that appeals (beautiful woodwork, ceiling medallions, and seven original stained glass windows), but Merrickville itself is a good getaway spot, with its restaurants, antique shops and attractive location on the Rideau waterway. The hosts of this B&B, Derry and Kathy Thompson, not surprisingly, count cooking and antiques among their interests. They also like to keep the place clean, so you'll be asked to remove your shoes. They'll provide gripper sox if you like – a good idea considering the shiny hardwood floors.

Upstairs, each of the guest rooms has its own bathroom. The second-floor Rideau Room, done in a blue, rose and white, has two single four-poster beds and an en suite bathroom with shower. Across the hall, the Empire Room is romantically furnished with a queen-size antique bedroom set. This room's bathroom, down the hall, has a tiled shower and whirlpool – both big enough for two. There's a $10 charge for the whirlpool, but for that price the hosts supply bath salts, champagne glasses,

special towels (!) and an ice-filled bucket. Then there's my favourite, The Georgian Suite. It has a queen-size four-poster bed, separate sitting room *and* a private bathroom.

The other rooms are on the the third floor. The queen-bedded Victoria Room has a turret and sloped ceilings, with a washbasin and cast-iron tub right in the room, but behind a Victorian screen for privacy. There's a two-piece next door. Across the hall, the plank-floored Canadiana Room has a four-poster king-size bed. There's another on-view cast-iron tub, with privacy curtain, which shares an alcove with a basin. But be warned all you tall types who want this room for its king-size bed – the en suite two-piece bathroom, with sloped ceiling, is *very* small.

And here's an idea for dinner. The Thompsons have teamed up with the nearby Baldachin Restaurant and for $135 a couple (*excluding* tip and taxes) you get your room, dinner with wine, plus breakfast, perhaps French toast or citrus crepes, complete with champers and OJ.

An elaborate place in a lovely historic town. One guest bedroom is a favourite with honeymooners, probably because of certain amenities in the bathroom.

145

L'Auberge du Marché

Nicole Faubert and Jean-Jacques
Charlebois
87 Guigues Ave.
Ottawa, ON K1N 5H8
613-241-6610

Best time to call: 7 AM to 9 PM
Besides English: French
Season: all year
Rates: S $54-85, D $64-85, $25
per additional person (plus GST)
Restrictions: no smoking, no
guests' pets
Facilities: 3 bedrooms; 1
bathroom shared only by guests
(combined shower/tub); 1 suite
with private bath (combined
shower/tub); central air
Parking: for 2 cars in backyard,
legal overnight on street
Breakfast: full
In residence: 2 young teen-agers
Location: Byward Market area,
10-minute walk to Parliament Bldgs.
Directions: take Nicholas St exit
from The Queensway (Hwy 417).
Keep left and take Dalhousie.
Turn left on St. Patrick. At next
light turn right on Parent. Turn
right on Guigues, the next street

If you're somewhat tentative about B&B,
L'Auberge du Marché is a good place to
stay because there's more privacy than
usual. This renovated turn-of-the-century
house, is divided in half and joined by
French doors at the entry hallways. One
side serves as the B&B, and the other is
occupied by Nicole and Jean-Jacques, and
their two young children. It's exceptionally
clean, attractively decorated and has an
excellent location.

Location means the Byward Market – a
small-scale commercial area containing
everything from trendy restaurants to hip
boutiques. It also means a short walk to
the Parliament buildings and downtown.
And just one block to the National Gallery.

If you're craving complete privacy, book
the self-contained suite on the main floor;
good value for two to four people. It has a
sitting room furnished with a floral queen-
size sofa bed and two cushioned chairs.
Through the French doors, you'll find a
bedroom with a queen-size brass bed.
There's also a kitchen and private bathroom.

The three bedrooms are on the second
floor. The back room is done in pink, and
has a queen-size brass bed with two chairs.
Another lace-curtained, smaller, room has
a double brass bed and antique dresser.
The bright master bedroom at the front is
furnished with a writing desk, two cushioned chairs and a queen-size four-poster
bed. The three bedrooms share a bathroom on the same floor. Just be aware
though, there is no common area for
guests to get together.

Breakfast is taken in the family dining
room. Weekdays you'll find the usual, but if
you're there Sunday, Nicole serves something special like crepes. And if you're a
first-time B&Ber, you shouldn't be feeling
tentative anymore.

L'Auberge du Marche

There's a lovely self-contained suite in this B&B that's good value for two to four people.

147

Brighton House Bed & Breakfast

André and Phyllis Parker
308 First Avenue
Ottawa, ON K1S 2G8
613-233-7777
E-mail: brighton.bb@sympatico.ca

Best time to call: after 10 AM
Languages: French
Season: all year
Rates: S $75-80, D $80-90 (plus GST)
Cards: AMEX/MC/VISA/ENROUTE
Restrictions: children over 12 welcome, smoking on porch, no guests' pets
Facilities: 3 bedrooms (1 double, 2 queen); 3 en suite bathrooms (2 shower/tub, 1 shower); living room for guests; air conditioning and phones in rooms
Parking: off-street for 3 cars
Breakfast: full
In residence: Two teens, Emily and Andrew; Tigger, the ginger cat
Location: central, the Glebe
Directions: exit Hwy 417 at Bronson Ave S, turn left on Chamberlain, then right on Lyon and right on First Ave.

Inspired by a visit to a B&B in England's Brighton Beach, Phyllis Parker decided to leave the corporate world behind and start her own B&B in this solid Edwardian home in Ottawa's desirable Glebe neighbourhood. The first thing you notice as you drive up to Brighton House (named for its inspiration) is the fully-landscaped front garden. The trend continues out back where Phyllis and husband, André have created patios and stepped gardens. Here guests can enjoy breakfast in warmer weather or sit out in the evenings.

Inside, Phyllis and André have done a complete renovation with B&B in mind. Business travellers will find amenities such as desks, computer jacks, and discreetly hidden colour TVs. And all will appreciate the comfortable seating and good reading lights. The second-floor Magnolia Room has garden views and two wing chairs in a sitting area. The en suite bathroom includes a deep soaker tub with shower. Two other rooms share the third floor. The Maple Room has a queen-size cannonball bed snuggled into one of two dormer windows, and a chair upholstered in a green-and-burgundy plaid pulls the room's colours together. The en suite bathroom has a glass-enclosed shower. The Mulberry Room has dormer windows, a queen-size sleigh bed and neutral colours highlighted by touches of burgundy and blue. There's a shower and tub in the large en suite bathroom.

Downstairs, the guest living room adjoins the dining room and, beyond it, a small anteroom set up with a fridge, microwave and the makings for coffee and tea. For breakfast, you'll get your Vitamin C and baked goods (perhaps a coffee-cake) along with a main dish such as crepes, bacon-and-egg pie or fruit pancake. After, you can stroll out to Bank Street lined with interesting shops and a whole range of restaurants. As for everything else Ottawa has to offer, you'll find it's not far away.

- Brighton House -

Business travellers take note –
you'll find what you need here.
And tourists will appreciate the
well-appointed rooms too.

149

Chiron Cottage

Barbara and Michael Chamberlain
98 Stanley Avenue
Ottawa, ON K1M 1N9
613-741-7422 (Fax: 741-5164)
E-mail: chiron@sympatico.ca

Best time to call: anytime
Season: all year
Rates: S $55-65, D $60-70 (no taxes)
Cards: VISA
Restrictions: children over 6 OK, no smoking, no guests' pets
Facilities: 3 bedrooms (1 double, 2 queen); 1 en suite bathroom, 1 shared (both with shower/tub); library with phone for guests
Parking: off-street for 2 cars
Breakfast: full or continental
Location: central Ottawa; 15-20 minute walk to National Art Gallery, Parliament Hill and Byward Market
Directions: from Hwy 417, exit 117. Take Vanier Pkwy and cross St. Patrick/Beechwood intersection into Crichton St. Follow Crichton. Turn left on Union St. Go to Stanley Ave

London's loss is Ottawa's gain. Former owners of Chiron House B&B in London, Ontario, Barbara and Michael Chamberlain have followed Michael's medical career to Ottawa. Here they've opened the delightful Chiron Cottage B&B in a quiet residential area near the picturesque Minto bridge that takes you across the Rideau River to the heart of things Ottawan. (A note to B&B wannabees: London is ripe for a couple of *exceptional* B&Bs – Chiron House is sorely missed.)

Built in 1865 this English cottage-style house offers three rooms for B&B. Two overlook the back garden; the red-and-cream Rideau Room has a small TV and en suite bathroom while the Victoria Room, with a double cannonball bed, has its own wash basin. It shares a sky-lighted bathroom with the Minto Room. Done in soft greens, the Minto Room's calm feel is enhanced by botanical prints. There's also a writing desk and discreetly-placed TV. For a small surcharge Barbara will rent only

one of these last two rooms if you wish a private-use bathroom.

You'll find interesting antiques throughout the house, including fine examples of English porcelain which Barbara collects. She's retired now, but was an antique dealer for a number of years so has had access to some choice pieces. And when I commented on some drapes in the dining room I learned they were an early Laura Ashley fabric acquired by Barbara when the family lived in London, England, some twenty-five years ago.

Breakfast the next morning is taken in the cosy yellow dining room. It's often continental but, if you like, Barbara will obligingly make it full. I had a tasty cheese blintze; you might be offered a salmon quiche or eggs and bacon. Retire with a coffee to the cosy library or garden patio and contemplate your day. You're in a perfect spot to make the most of it.

- Chiron Cottage -

From the delightful Chiron Cottage you can easily walk to the National Gallery, the Parliament Buildings and the Byward Market.

151

Le Gite Park Avenue

Anne-Marie and Irving Bansfield
54 Park Ave.
Ottawa, ON K2P 1B2
613-230-9131

Best time to call: 9 AM to 10 PM
Besides English: French
Season: all year
Rates: S $55, D $75 (no taxes)
Cards: VISA/MC
Restrictions: no smoking, enquire about guests' pets
Facilities: 3 bedrooms (2 queen, 1 with 2 double beds); 3 bathrooms, 1 shared by guests; 1 shared with hosts (both combined shower/tub), 1 powder room en suite; living room for guests; air conditioners in bedrooms
Parking: on site for 2 guest cars, legal overnight on street
Breakfast: full
Location: 20-minute walk to Parliament
Directions: take Metcalfe St exit off Hwy 417. Turn right (east) on Argyle and go 1 block to Elgin St at traffic lights. Turn left on Elgin. First right is Park Ave.

B&Bs are called *gites* in France. So you shouldn't be surprised to learn that the ancestors of Le Gite Park Avenue host Anne-Marie Bansfield, came from Brittany. She grew up speaking French in a small prairie town in Manitoba. Anne-Marie left a social work job to run the B&B while husband Irving, who grew up in Trinidad, teaches math at the local community college.

This house was built in 1904, just when styles were switching over from ornate Victorian to somewhat understated Edwardian. Inside, it has a fireplace, ceiling medallions and elaborate woodwork up the stairway. The decor's light and airy, with such feminine touches as pretty duvets, cushions from La Cache, and Laura Ashley cotton lace curtains. Guest bedrooms have rocking chairs and desks with swivel chairs; handy if you're in Ottawa on business or to research your thesis at the National Archives, (which is

what guests here have been known to do).

The third-floor suite has two rooms and a bathroom which opens into either room, so it's convenient for families or friends who come together. The larger room has a queen-size bed and a single bed. The smaller a double bed. There are two more rooms on the second floor. With its brass double bed and antique three-quarter bed, one has more of a back-to-the-past mood than the other which has a queen-size bed and en suite 2-piece bathroom. They share a bathroom with the hosts on the same floor.

Anne-Marie serves breakfast in a sunny alcove off the kitchen. As we chatted, she made a tasty cheese omelet. The freshly-baked multi-grain bread was Irving's contribution. Delish.

Le Gîte Park Ave.

There's a bright, airy mood to this house and Anne-Marie will send you on your way with a nutritious breakfast.

153

Robert's Bed & Breakfast

Robert Rivoire
488 Cooper St.
Ottawa, ON K1R 5H9
613-563-0161
1-800-461-7889

Best time to call: 10 AM to 9 PM
Season: all year
Rates: S $54-78, D $64-78 (plus GST)
Restrictions: no children, no smoking in house, no guests' pets
Facilities: 3 bedrooms (2 double, 1 queen); 2 bathrooms (1 private with combined shower/tub, 1 shared only by guests with combined shower/tub); sitting room for guests; central air
Parking: single file in drive, legal overnight on street
Breakfast: full
Location: central, 10-minute walk to Parliament Buildings
Directions: on Cooper St between Kent and Lyon; obtain specific directions when booking

I first stayed at Robert's B&B a few years ago, though it wasn't this particular place. It was another, smaller house where you shared the bathroom with Robert. It was an enjoyable two-night stay with the eager-to-please Robert, but it wasn't quite private enough to feature in this book.

Now Robert's got the kind of B&B I like. It was built in the last century and has some lovely stained glass windows and high ceilings. He's on the third floor, guests are on the second. And guests have the use of an attractively-furnished sitting room, with a working fireplace.

The nicest room here is the large front bed-sitting room, with its own bathroom and a beautiful stained glass window. The carpeting is pale rose, and the duvet cover on the queen-size brass bed is in a soft green. The seating area has an antique wicker chesterfield and chair, upholstered in a pretty chintz. And it has its own balcony.

The other two bedrooms are more simply decorated, but they're good value at $64 for two people. The Garden Room has a double brass bed with a duvet. The larger Centre Room has a double bed and a table that can serve as a desk. They share a spotless bathroom, reminiscent of the '70s with its predominantly brown colour scheme.

Robert offers a choice of full or continental breakfast. You'll have it in the dining room amid a collection of art and antique prints. The dining room table is glass and marble, and you'll find yourself sitting on chairs that came from Robert's mother's church in Namur, Quebec. The church went modern 20 years ago and Robert lucked into the chairs.

- Robert's B & B -

There's an attractive bed-sitting room here. The decor's wicker and chintz and it has an en suite bath and balcony.

Pillars & Lace Bed & Breakfast

Bob and Lois Pilot
307 Maple Ave.
Pembroke, ON K8A 1L8
613-732-7674

Best time to call: 10 AM – 1 PM
Season: all year
Rates: S $45-50, D $55-60 (no taxes)
Restrictions: not suitable for children, smoking outside, no guests' pets
Facilities: 3 bedrooms (3 double); 3 bathrooms shared by guests only (1 full with shower/tub, 1 2-piece, and powder room on main floor); parlour, sun room for guests; telephone in upper hall
Parking: off-street for 3 cars
Breakfast: full or continental
Location: Pembroke is on the Ottawa River, approx. 1½ hrs W of Ottawa, 5½ hrs N of Toronto
Directions: at intersection of Hwys 17 & 41, exit Paul Martin Dr. which turns into River Rd. Cross over Mackay St., continue up hill to Maple Ave. Turn left to 2nd house on right past flashing light

This grand old turn-of-the-century Edwardian home *does* have pillars, and you *will* find some some lace inside, as the name promises, but that's not the half of it. Besides winning community recognition for the outstanding restoration, former Arctic residents Bob and Lois Pilot have displayed throughout their home a collection of Inuit and early-Canadian art, that on occasion attracts tour groups from Ottawa's National Gallery. Canadian-art aficionados will recognize names like Bland, Mathews, Cullen and Pilot. These last two are Bob's grandfather and uncle – hence the keen interest.

You'll find the three guest bedrooms on the second floor. All are large, with period furnishings that came with the house. Lois has made many of the lace curtains and chintz bed-coverings herself and she line-dries (and irons!) the white cotton linens for that impossible-to-duplicate feel and smell. The large fully-renovated bathroom was originally the maid's quarters. Here, chamber pot lids make for a decorative display

against the Etruscan-red walls. There's also a convenient 2-piece bathroom nearby and another tucked under the main staircase downstairs.

Besides being a talented seamstress, Lois shines at breakfast. She's always on the hunt for interesting recipes – here's a sample: scrambled eggs rolled in a thin crepe horn topped with herbed-tomato salsa. Or how about pancakes dusted with cinnamon sugar accompanied by a poached pear drizzled with cognac-laced yogurt.

After, your knowledgeable hosts (Bob actually grew up in Pembroke) will help you plan your day. Whether you're interested in antiquing, hiking, cross-country skiing, white-water rafting, or touring Algonquin Park just 45 minutes away, they'll have useful insider tips. They'll even pack a lunch and rent you their touring bikes if you like.

Pillars & Lace

*Satisfy your appetite for early
Canadian art – **and** breakfast!*

157

Drummond House

Claire and Rick Leach
30 Drummond St. E.
Perth, ON K7H 1E9
613-264-9175

Best time to call: anytime before 10 PM
Besides English: French
Season: all year
Rates: S $55, D $65-70 (no taxes)
Restrictions: children over 5 welcome, no smoking, no guests' pets
Facilities: 3 bedrooms (1 twin-bedded, 1 double, 1 queen); 3 en suite bathrooms (2 combined shower/tub, 1 shower only); living room for guests; ceiling fans in bedrooms
Parking: on site
Breakfast: full
In residence: Snowball and Ragdoll, the cats
Location: an hour's drive from Ottawa or Kingston, two hours east of Peterborough
Directions: from Hwy 7 turn onto Drummond St towards downtown Perth (coming from Ottawa turn left at 1st light; from Peterborough/Toronto turn right at 3rd light)

When you learn that Drummond House was built in 1836, you may *sense* that Perth has been around a long time. Your intuition's confirmed when you discover that nearby is what's reputed to be the oldest golf course in *Canada*. In fact, Perth is rich with early heritage homes, mostly stone like Drummond House, which lend an attractive ambiance to this town of 6,000 straddling the banks of the Tay River.

Inside, I would call this B&B home more renovated than restored, though there are some original features such as the pine floor in the living room. But, for sure, if you're fussy, this is the place to be. Everything's pristine and matching (hosts Claire and Rick Leach had help from a designer with the decorating) and all three guest bedrooms have ceiling fans, reading tri-lights, wall-to-wall carpeting and private en suite bathrooms.

My favourite, the peach-and-green Tayview, has country pine furniture with white iron-and-brass twin beds. But you won't go wrong with the Wicker Room, with its queen-size bed done in peach, white and green. Or the Deco, either. Its furnishings, including the double bed headboard, belonged to Claire's mother.

For breakfast Claire may offer waffles, French toast or bacon and eggs. *Or* her "special pancakes". If I were you, I'd skip the first three, fine though they may be, and take her up on the pancakes. That's what we did. I gobbled up six or seven of these scrumptious melt-in-the-mouth delights before calling a halt to the calorie march. Even then, I had to use all my willpower to resist those left on the serving plate.

158

– Drummond House –

The pristine rooms here all have private en suite bathrooms – and if that's not enough, just wait 'til you try Claire's "special pancakes".

Dundela

Elaine Orgill and daughter, Jenn
489 Gordon Ave.
Peterborough, ON K9J 6G7
705-743-7228

Best time to call: evenings
Season: all year
Rates: S $45, D $55 (no taxes);
enquire about long-term rates
Restrictions: no smoking,
enquire about guests' pets
Facilities: 2 bedrooms (1 double,
1 queen and single); 2 bathrooms
(1 shared only by guests
combined shower/tub, 1 en suite
2-piece); two sun rooms and
living room for guests; central
air; in-ground pool
Parking: 4 cars in double drive
Breakfast: full
In residence: Ashi, a slightly
confused cat who thinks he's a dog
Location: a 1¾-hour drive east of
Toronto
Directions: obtain when booking
(near Parkhill and Monaghan in
west end)

Host Elaine Orgill's sunny outlook and inclusive nature are the hallmarks of her B&B. Along with the warm welcome you'll find a beautiful home. The Georgian-styled Dundela is named after Elaine's ancestral home in Ireland. She and daughter Jenn, were the decorating team. The inviting living room, with its blue, green and apricot colour scheme, has down-filled sofas and wing chairs next to an electric fireplace. As well, Elaine often invites guest to join her in the cosy family room off the kitchen with TV and gas fireplace.

Upstairs, the two guest bedrooms are also nicely decorated. The largest room has a private 2-piece bathroom. It's done in a blue-and-pink chintz and has queen and single beds. The other room's decor is mauve, pink and blue with French lace curtains, striped wallpaper and a brass double bed. Both have tri-lights over the bed. (At last, a host who realizes people like to read with more than a 40 watt bulb.)

You'll have breakfast in the burgundy-and-blue dining room. By then you will feel like old friends. In fact, you may find yourself having your last coffee with Elaine by the large heated in-ground pool in the backyard. And *then* you may decide to take a swim. It's a hard place to leave.

160

You may find yourself lingering over coffee at Dundela, then taking a swim in the pool – with such agreeable hosts, it's a hard place to leave.

161

Elizabeth Davidson House

Dean Noack
520 Dickson St.
Peterborough, ON K9H 3K1
705-749-6960
1-888-417-1010
E-mail: dnoack@accel.net

Best time to call: anytime
Season: all year
Rates: S $50-55, D $55-65 (no taxes)
Restrictions: enquire about children, no smoking, no guests' pets
Facilities: 4 bedrooms (2 en suite, 1 shower only, 1 with hand-held shower/tub; 1 shared by 2 rooms with shower/tub; 2-piece on main floor); guests may use parlour, library, living room and outdoor patio; central air
Parking: in double driveway
Breakfast: full
In residence: Otter, an Aussie mix
Location: 3 blocks to downtown
Directions: from downtown, go north on Water St to McDonnel. Turn right and go to B&B at end on crest of hill

At one time, Elizabeth Davidson House must have commanded a splendid view over the town of Peterborough. No doubt the reason lumber baron Samuel Dickson, chose this site for the Italianate-style house he built for his daughter, Elizabeth, in 1877. Newer buildings obscure some of the view now, but the house itself is just as grand as it once was.

It didn't take long for host Dean Noack to decide on Elizabeth Davidson House for his new B&B venture in 1990. He didn't even have to do much to restore it, since all the original architectural features were in excellent condition.

The four guest bedrooms are upstairs. Two have private bathrooms, including the spacious master bedroom. Its mahogany Sheraton-style bed is king-size, and a couple of wing chairs offer relaxed seating near the gas fireplace. The other with private bath is a two-room suite. The small anteroom has an oak desk and two tub chairs, and the bedroom has a king-sized bed with antique headboard.

I stayed in a cove-ceilinged room with inlaid mahogany twin beds and pink drapes. Another bedroom has a queen-size bed covered with a handmade plum-and-white quilt. These last two rooms share a tin-ceilinged bath complete with clawfoot tub and old-fashioned shower head. The shower's *directly* overhead so plan on washing your hair, whether you want to or not.

The next morning at breakfast I met the other guests. They were all just discovering the B&B option and one Toronto couple bought my book on the spot. Didn't even want to wait for the soon-to-be-released new edition, so taken were they with B&B. Elizabeth Davidson House had won more converts.

- Elizabeth Davidson House -

A lumber baron built this house for his daughter. It was, and is, one of the grand old houses of Peterborough.

163

Stepping Stone

Madeleine Saunders
328 Centreville Rd.
R.R. 2 Westport, ON K0G 1X0
613-273-3806

Best time to call: anytime
Besides English: French
Season: all year
Rates: S $60, D $80, luxury rooms $115-150 for two (no taxes)
Cards: VISA
Restrictions: older children welcome, smoking on porches only, no guests' pets
Facilities: 6 bedrooms (1 twin-bedded, 5 queen); 5 bathrooms (1 combined shower/tub shared with guests, 1 en suite with tub only, 3 en suite Jacuzzi); solarium for guests; central air
Parking: plenty on site
Breakfast: full
In residence: Candy, the dog; and 5 cats, Leo, Bandit, Lucky, Lotus and Angel
Location: a 35-minute drive north of Hwy 401 at Kingston
Directions: on Perth Rd 10, 3 kms south of Westport, watch for Centreville Rd. Turn west and go 2 kms

When Madeleine Saunders bought this house, it was open to the elements and home to wild creatures of every sort. But with unerring vision she transformed this 1840s stone house into an elegant country estate. It comes complete with a spring-fed pond, 150 bucolic acres and a few cows and horses in the nearby pastures.

It's an intelligent restoration, combining old and new. And the guest bedrooms are no exception. For a singular experience, reserve the large bedroom facing west. Its en suite bathroom is cleverly tucked under the eave. It's a mite cramped, but if you leave the bathroom door open you can enjoy the view over the countryside while soaking in the old-fashioned tub.

The Honey Room is named after the flowering locust tree outside the window. The twin room is furnished in antiques and the beds are covered with down-filled duvets in a blue-and-white pinstripe. These two share a bathroom.

Then there's the *pièce de résistance* – one of the most expensive rooms in this book at $150 for two, its grand proportions suit the floor-to-ceiling fireplace. French doors open to the outside, and it has a sitting area plus bathroom with oval Jacuzzi for two – *and* mood lighting. Two other luxury rooms with Jacuzzi en suites are also available.

At breakfast the next morning, Madeleine served us blueberry tea-biscuits and a tasty vegetable omelette made with eggs, fresh from a neighbouring farm. But it's just as likely to be pancakes with bacon and maple syrup, or poached eggs with Holandaise sauce and asparagus.

If you like breakfast, you may be interested to know Madeleine can cater anything from an intimate gathering of your closest friends (she's licensed by the LLBO) to a *marquee* wedding for 200. As well, she's a human resources consultant who works out of her home for clients in Ottawa. What with computers and fax she has the best of both worlds: a city career and a country lifestyle – an ideal setup for the nineties.

- Stepping Stone -

It took unerring vision to transform this abandoned wreck into an elegant country estate.

Richmond Manor

Pam and Bob Richmond
16 Blake Street
Barrie, ON L4M 1J6
705-726-7103
E-mail:
richmond.manor@sympatico.ca

Best time to call: anytime
Season: all year
Rates: S $50-60, D $65-75 (no taxes)
Restrictions: no smoking, no guests' pets
Facilities: 2 bedrooms (1 double, 1 queen); 1 bathroom shared by guests only (shower/tub), 1 shared with host (2 pce); common area on 2nd floor for guests; ceiling fans in all rooms; telephone on 2nd floor
Parking: off-street for many cars
Breakfast: full
In residence: 1 teenager, Matthew
Location: on the edge of downtown, close to Barrie's waterfront
Directions: from 400, take exit 96 (Dunlop St.) and travel 3 km E to Blake St. First house on left

On your way north? In Barrie on business? Skiing nearby? Whatever the reason, Richmond Manor is a handy B&B to know about. Hosts Pam and Bob Richmond lucked into this Georgian-styled home, backed by woods, and fulfilled their dream to start a B&B. Centrally located, in an older section of town, it's in a perfect spot. I was able to walk to a restaurant where I had an excellent meal while gazing out over Kempenfelt Bay, with lights from the odd high-rise gleaming across the water.

Former owners of Richmond Manor have included a Mayor and a Judge and, yes, it has the kind of features you'd expect – gracious principal rooms, and upstairs a large hall off which you'll find the two guest bedrooms and cosy sitting area with TV and magazines. The bedrooms are a good size, both have windows with lace balloon curtains and, in each, you'll find fine examples of Pam's tole painting. The Lafayette Room is the largest with a queen-size cherry four-poster bed plus a couple of Bergere chairs, a plum leather wing chair *and* a gas fireplace. The Williamsburg Room is done in peach, teal and white with a homespun bedspread on its double brass bed. References to Williamsburg are found in Pam's art and a hand-hooked rug.

Next morning, breakfast is in the formal dining room. Along with juice you'll have something like ruby-red poached pears or fresh berries, perhaps followed by whole wheat pancake with honeyed apple slices. I had a bacon-cheese casserole, followed by a sour cream apple coffee cake. I was impressed. It was Sunday night in the off-season and they had no idea they were having a guest (let alone a critic) until I knocked on the door at 9 that night. After breakfast, the Richmonds can tell you about the area's attractions – I was interested in a self-guided walking tour of Barrie's historical homes. Next time.

166

- Richmond Manor -

A surprising find in a lovely setting near Barrie's Kempenfelt Bay.

Banks Bed & Breakfast

Doug and Donna Banks
428 Beaumont Drive
R.R. 4
Bracebridge, ON P1L 1X2
705-645-2197

Best time to call: 8-9 AM or
6-11 PM
Season: all year
Rates: S $30, D $60, extra person
$30 (no taxes)
Restrictions: children over 10
welcome, no smoking, no guests'
pets
Facilities: 3 bedrooms (1 twin-
bedded, 1 double, 1 queen); 1
bathroom shared by guests only
(combined shower/tub); living
room for guest use
Parking: plenty on site
Breakfast: full
In residence: Domi, the corgi;
and Kayla, the cat
Location: a 2-hour drive north of
Toronto
Directions: exit from Hwy 11 to
Hwy 118 west. Go to traffic lights.
Turn left onto Beaumont Dr.

Just because a B&B isn't mentioned in *Best Places* doesn't mean you should give it a pass. Let me explain. I discovered this place while scouting possibilities for a previous edition of this book. I'd driven up, liked the outside, but no one was home. There *is* only one of me, and Banks B&B fell victim to the convoluted logistics of my research – I didn't get back to stay until I was doing the next edition.

Why go into all this? Well, after breakfast, when I told host Donna Banks who I was and that I wanted her B&B in my book, she told me a story about something that happened the year before. Donna works in a shop on Bracebridge's main street, and one day a couple of customers lamented that the B&B they wanted was booked. Donna said she knew of a nice B&B. It was hers. Holding *Best Places* aloft, the women asked, "Is it in this book?" On hearing "no," they said they'd only stay in places I recommended!

Now, I appreciate their trust, but those two missed out on a good spot. And just so this doesn't happen to you – if a promising B&B is *not* mentioned in this book, go have a look. Any good host is happy to show you around. *Then* decide whether to stay.

This house is a reproduction Georgian-style set high atop a wooded hill overlooking the scenic Muskoka River. It's tastefully decorated with a mix of old and new. Upstairs, the largest guest bedroom has a queen-size bed and a view over the river. Another smaller room, with a double bed, has roses as a theme. The twin-bedded room is simply decorated with white bedspreads and touches of blue and red.

Bacon and eggs were offered for breakfast, but I liked the sound of the other choice – fresh blackberry pancakes with strawberry butter. My instincts were right. I can *still* taste them.

- Bank's B&B -

Banks B&B sits high atop a wooded hill overlooking the scenic Muskoka River.

Tree Tops

Merle and Ron Bezoff
1015 Melandaw Lane, Box 334
Bracebridge, ON P1L 1T7
705-645-6271

Best time to call: 10 AM – 10 PM
Languages: some French, Ukrainian
Season: May – Oct. (enquire about other times)
Rates: S $45-80, D $65-95 (no taxes)
Restrictions: enquire about children; smoking outside, no guests' pets
Facilities: 3 bedrooms (1 twin-bedded, 1 queen, 1 king); 1 en suite bathroom (shower only), 1 shared by guests (shower/tub), 1 shared with hosts (2 pce); sitting areas for guests
Parking: off-street 3-4 cars
Breakfast: full
In residence: Button the cat (kept out of guest area)
Location: 10 min W of Bracebridge
Directions: from Hwy 11 go W on Hwy 118 to Beaumont Dr. Turn left. Follow Marina signs for 7.8 km. Turn left at Melandaw Lane

Following my invitation to long-time-summer-resident and Tree Tops host, Merle Bezoff, to be in this book, I received a lovely note. Speaking of her B&B, Merle wrote, "It's my labour of love and my attempt to share with others my little heritage in Muskoka which I am privileged to caretake for a few more years". That says it all. A warm and caring host who treats guests like good friends – by the time you leave, and Merle's snapped your photo for her album, you'll be the one who feels privileged.

Recently retired from education, Merle together with husband Ron, decided to open this chalet-style cottage to B&B guests. And, yes, you really are in the tree tops – it's quite an experience sitting on one of their balconies. Two of the bedrooms even have them. The fresh green-and-white Pine Room, with king-size bed and en suite bathroom has French doors opening onto one. As well, the twin-bedded Birch Room, with cream-and-mauve flowered comforters, has access to a balcony just outside its door. The pink-and-green Oak Room has a queen-size bed with rocking chair by a window overlooking mature oak and pine trees and the lake beyond. All rooms are carpeted, have comfortable beds, original paintings and good reading lights.

Your arrival is occasion for the Bezoffs to offer you refreshments and get you settled in. They *want* you to have the Muskoka cottage experience, so you'll find lots of cottagey things to do; reading, dock-sitting, trail-walking and slightly further afield, tennis courts, golf courses, boat cruises, and summer theatre.

Next morning, breakfast will probably be taken on the large main deck, and Merle will offer something like baked French toast or an egg-and-vegetable bake accompanied by smoked trout. Chef Ron cooks on weekends (he's still working during the week) – *his* specialty is wild blueberry pancakes with local maple syrup.

- Tree Tops -

A Muskoka cottage experience, nonpareil.

Beacon Inn B&B

Chris and Jim Kersey
5 Mitchell St.
Bruce Mines, ON P0R 1C0
705-785-9950
E-mail: Kerz@earthling.net

Best time to call: anytime in summer, otherwise evenings
Season: May-Oct
Rates: S or D $70-90 (no taxes)
Cards: VISA
Restrictions: not suitable for children, smoking outside only, no guests' pets
Facilities: 4 bedrooms (1 twin-bedded, 3 doubles); 4 en suite bathrooms (3 shower only, 1 shower and whirlpool tub; also 2-piece bathroom on main floor); Great Room and verandah for guests; central air
Parking: plenty on site
Breakfast: full
Location: 40-minute drive east of Sault Ste. Marie
Directions: at Museum in Bruce Mines turn S on Taylor St. Turn immediately right onto Mitchell

I was getting pretty blasé by the time I got to Bruce Mines up near the Soo. I'd been on the road for more than three months and I'd found some great new B&Bs. But corny as it sounds, this was the *only* time that I've actually had goose bumps. Part of it was coming across a terrific B&B when I *least* expected to. And part of it was finding a guest bedroom that really *spoke* to me.

Chris and Jim Kersey literally built around this old house, so not much of the original structure can be seen – outside *or* inside. You come in by way of a large entrance hall that leads to a high-ceilinged Great Room surrounded by floor-to-ceiling French windows looking out on picturesque Bruce Bay. There's a sitting area for guests around the working fireplace, and another part of the room is used for breakfast.

Upstairs, the decor of the four guest bedrooms, all with private bath, is inspired by the seasons. The pretty blue-and-white Summer Room is the one for romantics – it has a whirlpool bath. The Fall Room has hunter-green walls, warm pine floors and a high maple bed from Jim's parents. The Spring Room, with twin canopy beds, is done in yellow, pink and lilac. As for the Winter Room, it was the one I couldn't resist. Its bed coverings and balloon blinds are done in red tartan, trimmed with fabric in a bold black-and-white stripe. A red rocker sits by the window and pictures of winter scenes decorate the walls. And don't fret about which room to pick for the vista – you can see the bay from any of them.

There's so much more to tell. About the pleasingly different breakfast, the nightly rum cake ritual, the outdoor spa on the verandah overlooking the bay and the lively personalities of this young couple. Then there's Bruce Mines' stock of heritage architecture, admittedly small, but interesting nonetheless.

- Beacon B & B -

A treasure. A jewel. Call it what you will. This B&B had me in a tizzy.

Doorknob Inn

Frances and Dick Fraser
R.R. 4, #7231
Stayner, ON L0M 1S0
705-428-5761

Best time to call: 9 AM – 9 PM
Languages: some Japanese
Season: all year
Rates: S $55-65, D $60-70 (no taxes)
Cards: VISA
Restrictions: enquire about children 8 & older, no guests' pets
Facilities: 3 bedrooms (1 twin-bedded or king, 2 double); 1 en suite bath (shower only), 2 shared (shower/tub, 2 pce); living room and parlour for guests; room fans; phone available
Parking: ample off-street
Breakfast: full
In residence: Biz, Spooke and Luckie, the cats
Location: 7 mins S of Collingwood E of Hwy 24
Directions: go to first road N of Duntroon flashing light (at intersection of Hwys 91 & 24). Turn E on 27/28. Go 1.5 kms to third house on south side.

After ten years of weekend-commuting from their Toronto home to restore this Victorian farm house, Frances and Dick Fraser finally got to move in full-time. Frances left her CBC production job to run the delightful Doorknob Inn, as they've called their B&B, but Dick still commutes – this time in the opposite direction.

Judging by the imaginative name, I was betting this was a B&B I'd like. (Though one can never tell!) From the moment I walked in and saw the keeping room with its Vermont stove, and heard the Maritime lilt in Frances' voice, I was hooked.

The three bedrooms upstairs are equally attractive. The Green Room has an en suite bathroom with large shower unit and heat lamp. The double brass bed has a white crocheted spread from Ireland and cream moiré wallpaper scattered with roses. The other two bedrooms share a bathroom, but the blue-and-rose Backstairs Room with its double iron-and-brass bed also has access down the back stairs to a two-piece wash-room. The twin-bedded (or king) Pipe Room has two windows facing Blue Mountain and the walls are an historic peach and the woodwork's painted green. Each room features some memento of the Frasers' native Nova Scotia – perhaps a hooked rug, log cabin quilt or feather-painted pine dresser.

Next morning, you'll have breakfast in the pine-floored dining room with original tin ceiling. Frances likes to cook so she always comes up with something special. You might start with a fruit course of local apples with orange-Cointreau glaze in a pool of French vanilla yogurt. Or poached pears with maple syrup laced with brandy. Then, perhaps, baked French toast with an interesting topping or individual baked omelettes with smoked salmon on the side. After, hike or cross-country ski from the Frasers' side door or be on your way to explore everything this popular four-season tourist area has to offer.

– The Doorknob Inn –

A warm Maritime welcome in a cosy Ontario farmhouse.

An Alternative Bed & Breakfast

Cathie and Glen Simmons
595 Hotchkiss Street
Gravenhurst, ON P1P 1H8
705-687-2085
E-mail: gsimmons@muskoka.net

Best time to call: 10 AM – 10 PM
Languages: some Japanese
Season: all year
Rates: S $60-75, D $70-85 (no taxes)
Cards: VISA/MC
Restrictions: children welcome, smoking outside, no guests' pets
Facilities: 3 bedrooms (2 double, 1 queen); 1 en suite bathroom (shower/tub), 1 shared by guests (shower/tub); living room for guests; portable phone
Parking: ample
Breakfast: full
In residence: young son, Micah; Brilly, the standard poodle
Location: 76 kms N of Toronto
Directions: from Hwy 11 take Hwy 169 exit to Bethune Dr. At 1ˢᵗ lights, turn W. At next lights (Muskoka Rd S), turn left. Take 1ˢᵗ street on right to last house on left

You'll find this contemporary home three blocks from downtown Gravenhurst, flanked by woods and meadows. As you climb the entrance steps, you may note some statuary that's just a little different from the usual – turns out hosts Glen and Cathie Simmons shipped these stone temple gods back from Bali. And that's only the beginning of the "alternative" experience you're about to have.

Inside, the Simmons have collected exotic textiles and artifacts from Asia and Africa which make for a dramatic display in the cathedral-ceilinged living room. Nearby, the sleeping wing contains three guest bedrooms with wooden furnishings crafted by the talented Glen and stained in vivid hues. As for the comfort of the futon beds, I was off to dreamland in no time, tucked between the all-cotton sheets.

This multi-faceted couple have many fascinating stories to tell, as does their articulate young son, Micah. Cathie, when not hosting B&B, is either in Ottawa, or travelling the world doing international development. Glen's a yoga instructor and a papier maché artist, with work in galleries across Canada.

When I showed up for breakfast next morning, Glen was playing some gentle reggae music from his native Caribbean, and I detected a faint hint of incense in the air. Not objectionable, just surprising. (As with everything else here, there was a story involving India and Glen's search for the world's best incense. But I'll let him tell it.) I chose a standard-issue Canadian breakfast, but for the adventurous, the menu offers Balinese black rice pudding and freshly made miso shiru.

This is a perfect B&B for a group – have an early morning yoga session, take a papier maché class in Glen's studio downstairs or else plan your day with the Simmons' help.

– An Alternative Bed & Breakfast –

*Come with a sense of adventure
and prepare to be wowed.*

177

All Hart

Heather Alloway and Barry Hart
R.R. 2
Haliburton, ON K0M 1S0
705-457-5272 (phone/fax)

Best time to call: early AM to 10 PM
Languages: French
Season: all year
Rates: S or D $95 Extra person $25 (no taxes)
Cards: VISA
Restrictions: no children, no smokers, no guests' pets
Facilities: 3 bedrooms (1 twin, can be king, 1 queen, 1 king); 3 en suite bathrooms (2 shower only and 1 Jacuzzi/shower); private lounge for guests; telephone in lounge
Parking: off-road for 4 cars
Breakfast: continental
Location: 2½ hrs from Toronto, 50 mins from Algonquin Park, 1 hr E of Bracebridge
Directions: from Haliburton village, drive 3 km S on County Rd 1. Turn right on S Kashagawigamog Rd. Proceed 2 km to B&B opposite golf course

Pioneers settled here in the 1860s when the closest supplies were a canoe-and-portage trip away in Minden. The Borden family cleared the land, but settled for logging when the hoped-for farming venture was doomed by bedrock. Later, in the 1930s, their descendants opened a golf course. Summer visitors came in a mahogany launch to play the rustic links. But in 1949, exhausted by the back-breaking work, the Bordens went on to other things leaving their granite farmhouse behind to slowly deteriorate. That is, until another set of pioneers came along 40 years later.

Former Torontonians, Heather Alloway and Barry Hart took to the challenge with the same dedication and hard work as their predecessors. They poured their hearts into the restoration plus construction of a new separate wing for guests. The name All Hart B&B besides being a reference to the spirit needed to undertake the daunting task (and a delightful play on their names), is indicative of what guests can expect here.

Inside, you'll find large, nicely decorated bedrooms, all with en suite bathrooms. Heather is partial to bold chintzes in darker colours and everything matches. The bright common area for guests is comfortably furnished, and a Vermont wood stove provides cosy warmth for winter hikers and cross-country skiers. As well, many guests are taking courses at the Haliburton School of Fine Arts. In summer, you'll find folks down at the dock, with drink in hand, taking in the restorative view. Or you'll find them across the road at that old golf course, now one of the finest in the area. And, of course, there's Fall – I was there at the height of the colours and it was absolutely brilliant.

Heather brings breakfast into the guest wing. She calls it 'gussied-up continental' – always fresh fruit, a cold cereal buffet, and something home-baked such as scones, muffins or coffee cake. By then, you'll be feeling like pampered guests, no pioneering for you.

—All-Hart Bed & Breakfast—

A four-season B&B tucked away in the Haliburton Highlands.

Steinwald

Don and Vonnie Robinson
R.R. 4
Lion's Head, ON N0H 1W0
519-795-7894

Best time to call: anytime
Season: all year
Rates: S $45, D $60 (no taxes)
Restrictions: limited smoking, enquire about guests' pets
Facilities: 3 bedrooms (2 double, 1 double and single); 2 bathrooms, (1 combined shower/tub shared with hosts, 1 2-piece bathroom shared only by guests); living room shared with hosts
Telephone: in living room plus portable
Breakfast: full
Location: on Bruce Peninsula between Wiarton and Tobermory
Directions: on Hwy 6, go 8 kms north of Ferndale. Turn right at Lindsay Rd 5 and go 4 kms to East Rd. Turn left on paved road past St. Margaret's Church, then gravel road to just past Cape Chin Road North (7 kms total from Hwy 6)

It's not often that you're offered a pioneer log cabin at a garage sale. When it happened to Vonnie and Don Robinson, they didn't hesitate. What transpired is this. The owner was having a contents sale. Don and Vonnie dropped by, but they weren't interested in the contents. They wanted the house. They told the owner that if he was interested in selling, they'd buy. He was. The original log cabin has been restored and added to and now it's decorated with antiques and local crafts.

The guest bedrooms are in the pioneer vein. Two on the second floor share a 2-piece bath upstairs, and a full bathroom with the Robinsons downstairs. (If you want a shower, it's slightly awkward – when we stayed, we had to squeeze past some early diners to get to the bathroom.)

If you like to waken to the morning sun, the South Room's for you. Just leave the white eyelet curtains open when you go to bed. It's decorated in shades of blue and has an easy chair. The North Room is done in blue and sunny yellow. It has a double and single bed. Both rooms have carpeting on the floors. The third is a sleeping cabin, with a double bed, shaded by a century-old apple tree at the back of the garden. Guests staying there also share the home's main floor bathroom.

Predictably, for this part of the province, Don and Vonnie are nature-lovers. They have 100 acres and eagerly share its pleasures; birds, flowers, and unusual rock formations. Don's always game for a hike – have him show you some of the rare orchids on the property. For a longer hike, the Bruce Trail is nearby. I was enthralled by a visit to a now-famous garden called Larkwhistle, which is about 10 minutes away by car.

And who knows. You may find something interesting at a garage sale.

- Steinwald -

The Robinsons have 100 acres of property and eagerly share its pleasures with their guests. If you like, Don will take you on a hike to see the rare orchids that grow there.

181

Rockville Inn B&B

Carol and Ron Sheppard
R.R.1
Mindemoya, ON P0P 1S0
705-377-4923

Best time to call: 4:30–10:30 PM
Season: all year
Rates: S 65, D 75 (Jul 1 - Sep 1)
Off-season S $50, D $60 (no taxes)
Cards: MC
Restrictions: smoking outside, no guests' pets
Facilities: 4 bedrooms (all queen); 4 en suite bathrooms; living room with fireplace for guests; telephone in kitchen
Parking: off-street for 4 cars
Breakfast: full
Location: 40 mins from ferry dock South Baymouth, 30 mins from Little Current bridge
Directions: obtain when booking

The Rockville Inn is my pick of Manitoulin Island's B&Bs, even though it doesn't meet the strict rule I follow for the other B&Bs in this book, in that the hosts don't live in it. Carol and Ron Sheppard were living in their newer house nearby, when it struck them that perhaps they could fix up Ron's folks' place, then empty, for B&B guests. Their perseverance paid off with a completely refurbished B&B done in a casual country style.

The rooms are all decorated around different themes. The Navaho is done western style, Irene has country taste, the Lane Gail is a done in a feminine floral and the Maple has maple leaf motifs on its sheets and stencilled walls. Knowing European preferences, The Sheppards have provided two rooms Euro-style with *all* bathroom facilities right in the room. Thankfully, there are also two other rooms better suited to most of us uptight North Americans, with standard three-piece bathrooms en suite. It's your pick.

Breakfast the next morning was taken overlooking the calm waters of Lake Manitou, the largest freshwater lake on an island in the world. Carol's off to work weekdays, so she gets things organized and her friend Gail comes in to look after guests. Gail's friendly enthusiasm got us off to a good start for a day of exploring magical Manitoulin. There are excellent walking trails, easy cycling through pastoral countryside, canoeing on clear inland waters, and some of the best yachting anywhere. And it's well-known far beyond Canada's borders. Come summer, tourists arrive by the score to soak up the special ambiance.

And here's a thought – why not book this B&B for a group-stay in the off-season. (There's a separate self-contained apartment they rent out as well, boosting to twelve the number who can sleep here comfortably.) The magic doesn't leave, just the tourists.

182

- Rockville Inn -

Why follow the crowd; come in the off season and have magical Manitoulin to yourselves.

183

Irish Mountain B&B

John Avery
R.R. 1
Meaford, ON N4L 1W5
519-538-2803
E-mail: hugo@log.on.ca

Best time to call: anytime
Besides English: some French
Season: all year
Rates: Jul & Aug: S or D $65-95
Other times: S or D $45-75 (no taxes)
Restrictions: children welcome, smoking outside only, enquire about guests' pets
Facilities: 3 bedrooms (2 queen and single, 1 queen only); 3 guest bathrooms (2 en suite with shower/tub; 1 en suite with shower); living room, deck, pool and hot tub; central air
Parking: on site
Breakfast: full
In residence: Slick, the cat; Maddie the German shepherd, who stays in host quarters
Location: a good 2-hour drive northwest of Toronto's northern limits
Directions: on Hwy 26 drive 5 kms west of Meaford. Turn north on Grey Rd 112 (9th line). Go 5 kms to top of hill. Turn left to 1st house on left

What you *don't* see in the sketch opposite is what you get here – a magnificently panoramic view. And the best place to see it is from the top-level Lakeview Suite. Though pricier than the other rooms, it's worth the extra loonies. Lofty cathedral ceilings set the airy tone. The light neutral decor effectively offsets the boldly coloured painting over the bed. There's an en suite bathroom *plus* a sun room with 3 skylights and tripod-mounted telescope.

Back on the main floor, the two other bedrooms, though smaller, are nicely furnished, and each has an en suite bathroom. Your best bet here is to opt for the Bay Room which has the better view.

The large living room with comfy, curvy furniture, has TV, VCR and wood-burning fireplace. Off to one side there's a hot tub placed to take in the sights, and outside there's an enormous deck plus swimming pool.

Bobbie and John Avery built this home in 1989. Bobbie's the Toronto Star's area correspondent, while John does property management and runs the B&B. Next morning, John provided a substantial breakfast of grain waffles with walnuts, taken while overlooking a meadow bright with goldfinches snacking precariously on seed-pods, I later accompanied John and his German Shepherds on their morning ramble (There's only one dog now).

If you're interested in a longer hike, John knows the nearby Bruce Trail well and will drop you off at one point and pick you up at another. Or for a different kind of adventure you could always charter his 22-foot sailboat, and sail out into Georgian Bay.

Just wait 'til you see the view.

Little Lake Bed & Breakfast

Jennifer Hart, Milton Haynes
and Brett Barber
669 Yonge St.
Midland, ON L4R 2E1
705-526-2750 (Fax 526-9005)
E-mail: little_lake.bb@csolve.net

Best time to call: anytime
Season: all year
Rates: S $60-$80, D $65-85 (no taxes)
Cards: VISA/MC
Restrictions: smoking outside, no guests' pets
Facilities: 4 bedrooms (1 twin-bedded, 3 queen); 2 en suite bathrooms (shower only); 2 private-use (1 shower only, 1 shower/tub); living room for guests; ceiling fans in bedrooms; telephone in dining room
Parking: off-street for 7 cars
Breakfast: full or continental
In residence: teenager, Brett; Rory, the cat
Location: in central Midland
Directions: from Hwy 400, take Hwy 93 N to Midland, turn right onto Yonge St.

I've had the back view of Little Lake B&B sketched, simply because the unprepossessing front gives no hint of what's inside. Pulling into the brick-paved parking area, surrounded by attractive landscaping, I saw what looks like a well-kept bungalow. I was welcomed by the self-assured teen son, Brett. The first two rooms, just inside the front door, were very clean and neat and nicely decorated. One, the twin-bedded Coral Room has a white, coral and green 'Bermuda' decor and private-use bathroom down the hall. The Green Room has an en suite bathroom and is completely set up for the business traveller with desk and computer port. Very handy. Then Brett led me to the rest of the house. Well!

Turns out the back half was originally a commercial building that got moved here from downtown, high ceilings and all. So the guest living room with 11-foot beamed ceiling and the two back bedrooms are completely different. One is the Rose Room with Queen-size bed, green wicker chairs and private-use bathroom. The other is the sunny yellow Century Room with private bathroom and its own entrance to the back deck. Besides the queen-size bed there's a double pull-out sofa. The hardwood floors and trim are original and large new windows offer views of Little Lake surrounded by parkland.

Next morning hosts Jennifer Hart, and Milton Haynes (if he's not off to his real estate job), serve breakfast by the fireplace, just behind all those windows you see in the sketch. It's usually continental with OJ, perhaps fresh fruit, baked apples or poached pears, a choice of several cereals and some kind of home baking such as scones or muffins. After, there's enough to keep you occupied for several days, what with the Martyrs' Shrine, Wye Marsh Wildlife Centre, Discovery Harbour and the like. Or you can walk to Huron Indian Village and the Huronia Museum, right from your hosts' back door.

- Little Lake B&B -

With all the tourist action in Midland, make sure you book well in advance here.

Satis House Bed & Breakfast

Jo-Anne Hynd
258 English Line
Powassan, ON P0H 1Z0
705-724-2187

Best time to call: evening
Languages: French, some Swedish
Season: all year
Rates: S $45-55 D $55-65 (no taxes)
Restrictions: children over 10 welcome, smoking outside, guests' pets in garage
Facilities: 3 bedrooms (1 twin-bedded, 1 double, 1 queen); 1 en suite bathroom, 1 shared by guests (shower/tub); living room for guests; telephone in living room
Parking: off-street for 8-10 cars
Breakfast: full
In residence: Smoky, the cat
Location: 25 mins south of North Bay, 3 ½ hrs N of Toronto
Directions: from Hwy 11, turn left onto English Line (approx 10 km N of Trout Creek)

I encourage hosts who think they have something special to offer to drop me a line – but I've learned you *never can tell*. I'd had an interesting letter from Satis House host Jo-Anne Hynd, so was intrigued to see what her place was actually like. She'd expressed a vision for her B&B which, she wrote, "reflects my personal philosophy that nature is the easiest way to soothe the spirit and soul."

As soon as we arrived, I knew this was a place for my book. Jo-Anne provided a warm and gracious welcome. And the house, in its natural setting, surrounded by meadows and distant woods, didn't seem forlorn, as it had appeared in the photo she'd sent. Inside, all is new and especially set up for B&B; a comfortable sitting room downstairs and upstairs, three guest bedrooms, all nicely decorated.

Jo-Anne runs the B&B and teaches Grade 2 French Immersion full time in North Bay – a busy gal, but one who still finds time to bake. And she's some baker.

On arrival you'll find a basket of her homemade cookies in your room. And at some point during your stay you're sure to be offered her famed butter tarts. As for breakfast, Jo-Anne makes outstanding muffins (we had orange/cranberry). As well, breakfast includes fresh fruit salad, OJ, and perhaps a quiche with crisp bacon and lightly seasoned potatoes.

Now, it's great to know about Satis House if you're going to be around North Bay, but for me it's one of the many perfect destination B&Bs in this guide – just make a point of booking in for a couple of days. You'll find lots to do with parks, lakes and golf-courses nearby. But do as Jo-Anne recommends. Slow down and just be.

A place to shift gears and just be.

Cavana House

Brenda and Bob Tuddenham
241 Mississaga St. W.
Orillia, ON L3V 3B7
705-327-7759

Best time to call: evenings
Season: all year
Rates: S $60, D $78 (no taxes)
Restrictions: children over 12 welcome, no smoking, no guests' pets
Facilities: 3 bedrooms (1 twin-bedded, 2 double); 3 en suite bathrooms (2 shower only; 1 combined shower/tub); living room for guests; central air
Parking: on site
Breakfast: full
Location: an hour and 15 minute's drive north of Toronto
Directions: from Hwy 11 north at Orillia, take Memorial Ave exit. Follow Memorial to the hospital (Mississaga St). Turn left. Go 1 block to house on left. Guest parking is to the right front of house

I'm not sure what it is about the guest soap here but I found myself washing my hands at every opportunity. Aromatic, with woodsy overtones, it's positively addictive. Not an unusual reaction, says Cavana House host Bob Tuddenham. When I wasn't sniffing soap, I was enjoying tea in the living room with our jovial host and other guests. Or examining pictures of Cavana House (pronounced like Cavanaugh) the way it used to be. Bob and Brenda Tuddenham (he's retired from Eaton's management and she's a school counsellor) are another pair who've used the B&B excuse to rescue a sad, old Victorian. It's a remarkable transformation.

Upstairs, the second and third-floor guest bedrooms are all bright, airy and attractive. Each has a TV. The double-bedded Victorian Room is the one favoured by many guests, mostly for its large bathroom with Jacuzzi and separate shower. The Rose Room, though, is my favourite with its wicker, white-iron double bed and lace curtains. Roses and ivy have been hand-painted (by a guest!) above the windows and the bathroom's pine floors are artfully stencilled as well. Then there's the Attic Room, reached by way of a steep flight of stairs. Spacious, with a sitting area and TV at one end, and a double brass bed at the other, it's done in wicker with a sunny yellow-and-rose chintz. There's also a daybed.

You'll take breakfast in the formal dining room furnished with antiques. Along with the usual, there'll be something like an omelette, French toast, or fruit pancake – Brenda likes to gives you a choice the night before, so you'll have something to ruminate about.

190

- Cavana House -

A soap to sniff – and a B&B to savour.

Seguin Country Inn Bed & Breakfast

Judy and Neil Ibbitson
R.R. 3, 115 North Rd.
Parry Sound, ON P2A 2W9
705-746-5911 (tel/fax)

Best time to call: anytime
Season: all year
Rates: S $65, D $75 (plus GST)
Restrictions: enquire about children, smoking outside, no guests' pets
Facilities: 6 bedrooms (1 king or twin-bedded, 1 double plus twin-bedded, 4 queen); 5 en suite bathrooms and 1 private-use (all shower/tub), main floor for guests; phone available
Parking: ample off-street
Breakfast: full
In residence: Marley, the dog; 1 outside smoker
Location: five minutes from downtown Parry Sound
Directions: N on Hwy 400 to Hwy 124, travel E for 1.6 kms to Burnside Bridge Rd. Turn right. Then turn right immediately onto North Rd. Go .6 km to B&B on left

With all the natural attractions in the Parry Sound area, and with the city being a natural stopover on your way north, Seguin Country Inn comes as pleasant happenstance. Hosts Judy and Neil Ibbitson have completely renovated an old farmhouse and built a huge addition especially for B&B. Before starting, Judy polled friends to find out what they looked for in a B&B. Topping the lists were large rooms and private bathrooms, followed by nice decor and great breakfasts. So that's what she's done.

It all looks pretty new when you drive up the lane curving through the well-treed grounds. On entering, you'll be in a large foyer decorated with a rich plum-coloured wall covering. Straight ahead, through a wall of windows, you'll note a hot tub and large deck, which guests are welcome to use. To your left, in the farmhouse part, you'll find a comfortable guest sitting area done country-style, with a wood-burning fireplace. And to your right, is the large

wheelchair-accessible Susan's Room, done in pink, burgundy and off-white. Upstairs, you'll find five more bedrooms, (featuring pictures of, and named after, their daughters) including the *huge* Leah's Room. Its bathroom is down the hall. The four other rooms have en suites and are all *very* big.

Next morning, Judy's breakfasts bring many compliments. For starters, there's always fruit or perhaps a nutty granola parfait with yogurt and preserves. She then comes up with main dishes such as ricotta-cheese pancakes or French toast Raphael (a casserole of fruit and cubed French bread with eggs, milk, cinnamon, cream cheese and dark maple syrup). After, avail yourself of the many activities. In summer take a 30,000-island boat cruise, visit Killbear Provincial Park, or, if you book well in advance, take in the world-renowned Festival of the Sound. Winter brings cross-country skiing and snowmobiling – extensive area trails go right across the Ibbotson's driveway.

— Seguin Country Inn —

Large rooms, private baths and great breakfasts, just like the hosts' friends advised.

DunRovin Bed & Breakfast

Wilsie and Bob Mann
Box 304
Port Carling, ON P0B 1J0
705-765-7317
E-mail: dunrovin@muskoka.com

Best time to call: afternoon/evening
Season: all year
Rates: S or D $80-90 (no taxes)
Restrictions: not suitable for children, no smoking, no guests' pets
Facilities: 2 bedrooms (1 twin-bedded, 1 queen); 2 bathrooms (shower only) 1 en suite and 1 nearby; sitting room near bedrooms for guests
Parking: off-street for 3 cars
Breakfast: full
Location: north end of Lake Muskoka, minutes from Bala, Port Carling
Directions: take Hwy 11 to Hwy 169 N or Hwy 118 to Hwy 169 S. Take Mortimer's Point Rd., drive 2 km to B&B

Whether you arrive by car, boat or float-plane, DunRovin B&B is a good spot to take a break from your own roving. Hosts Wilsie and Bob Mann bought this Viceroy-style home, surrounded by wildflower gardens, and retired here in the heart of their beloved Muskoka. You'll find the guest quarters on the lower level so they're quite separate from the Manns'.

From the cosy sitting area you enter the two guest bedrooms and, in winter, the cedar-panelled hot-tub room. One room overlooks the north bay of Lake Muskoka. Its twin iron beds are dressed in a green, pink and mauve chintz. Pine, oak and wicker furnishings give a cottagey feel and its private-use bathroom is nearby. The other room has a romantic half-canopy queen-size bed decorated with rose silk flowers. Its window looks out on wildflowers and forest out back and the bathroom's en suite.

Next morning, Wilsie (a diminutive of Wilson, which was not only her mother's *first* name, but her great-great-grandmother's as well) brings breakfast out to the spacious deck in good weather, or in the great room upstairs, in not-so-good. She's an old-fashioned kind of baker, with a sprinkling of heart-healthy, so it's sure to be good. Perhaps cranberry-blueberry pancakes or orange French toast, plus something like sticky buns or low-fat muffins.

Over breakfast, you'll learn that Bob and Wilsie share many interests; they're both pilots and they both love to work with wood. In fact, guests are intrigued to learn that together they've built an exact replica of a mahogany Dispro boat, common on the lake in the 1930s. Go have a look. And while you're down at the boathouse, you'll want to stay around for a swim in the shallow sandy waters. And after, pick any chair on top of the boathouse, sit back and relax and enjoy your clear view all the way down the bay.

194

— DunRovin Bed & Breakfast —

A Muskoka cottage experience with all the comforts of home, plus some...

195

Stone Cottage

Joanne and Bill Chalmers
R.R. 1
Port Sydney, ON P0B 1L0
705-385-3547

Best time to call: 9 AM to 9 PM
Season: all year
Rates: S $55, D $65 (no taxes)
Restrictions: children over 10 welcome, no smoking, no guests' pets
Facilities: 3 bedrooms (1 double-bedded, 2 queen); 1 bathroom shared only by guests (combined shower/tub); living room and sun room for guests; central air
Parking: plenty on site
Breakfast: full
In residence: Gabrielle and Jasmine, Siamese cats; Chelsea, the Wheaten terrier
Location: near Huntsville, a 2½ hour drive north of Toronto
Directions: from Hwy 11 go east on South Mary Lake Road in Port Sydney. Follow road to bridge. Cross bridge and turn right on Deer St. Go 1 km to B&B

Most of the nostalgia in this book is for old-house buffs. Now Stone Cottage certainly gives buffs a hit – built in 1880 of immense slabs of dressed granite, it's been updated for B&B by Joanne and Bill Chalmers. But there's nostalgia of another sort, too. Golfers will find links not too unlike those of the last century. A rustic nine holes cut a meandering swath through a section of the Chalmers' 32 acres of pine forest, bordering the North Muskoka River. Just be sure your swing's accurate. These fairways don't need artificial hazards, what with the rough closing in on both sides. Even if you're not a golfer, it's pleasant to follow the course down to the river.

You'll find Stone Cottage just outside the village of Port Sydney which bills itself as the heart of Muskoka – it's just a 20-minute drive north to Huntsville, or half an hour south to Bracebridge. Bill and Joanne have decorated with a mix of antiques and Canadiana-style furniture, with light wall-to-wall carpeting giving a contemporary feel. Guests are welcome to use the formal living room with its stone fireplace. Summertime, though, most gather in the comfy sun room finished in cedar and decorated with antiques.

The guest bedrooms are all upstairs. The spacious Homestead Room has a pine four-poster queen-size bed and is decorated in a rose and green floral wallpaper. The Rose Room, with its burgundy-and-pink wallpaper, has a pine four-poster double bed and the Blue Room has a queen-size iron-and-brass bed. All three rooms share a bathroom.

Breakfast is served up on Limoges china. We had cheese blintzes with fruit sauce, topped with yogurt and home-made granola, while light classics played in the background.

- Stone Cottage -

Golfers here can play on rustic
links which cut a meandering
swath through the pine forest. It
almost makes you want to don
plus fours.

197

The Willows Inn Bed & Breakfast

Linda and Paul Gordon
1 Main Street
Rossport, ON P0T 2R0
807-824-3389 (Fax 824-3492)
E-mail:
pgordon@schreiber.lakeheadu.ca

Best time to call: 7:30 AM – 10 PM
Season: all year
Rates: S $60-100, D $80-125
(plus GST) ask for off-season
Cards: VISA/MC
Restrictions: enquire about
children, smoking outside, well-
behaved guests' pets welcome
Facilities: 4 bedrooms (1 twin-
bedded, 3 queen, cot available); 4
en suite bathrooms (2 shower
only, 1 whirlpool tub/shower, 1
whirlpool tub/separate shower);
main floor for guests; fax,
computer and phone available
Parking: ample
Breakfast: full
In residence: Willi & Ami, the
Bichon Frisé dogs
Location: N shore of L Superior
on Hwy 17. 2 hrs E of Thunder
Bay, 6 hrs W of Sault Ste. Marie
Directions: centre of village

Right up front, let me tell you that I haven't been to The Willows Inn. I'd had good reports, but in my quest to visit 500 B&Bs and select 50 for this edition of the book, I just didn't have the time to go myself. But I *really* wanted to check it out. So what to do? In the end, I sent a mystery reviewer whose judgment I trusted. She and a friend stayed one night and sent a "two thumbs up" report. She used terms like "immaculate" and "fresh European decor with wood-burning fireplace in living room". As for breakfast, they "had juice, a delicious fruit compote laced with rum and lime, apple pie muffins, and cheese-rarebit eggs as a deliciously decadent finale (mmm!)" She did mention train noise but said, "the muffled sound was part of the charm". It was such an unambiguous vote of confidence that I phoned hosts Linda and Paul Gordon to invite them into the book.

In talking to Linda by phone I learned more about the guest bedrooms. All have sitting areas, en suite bathrooms and armoires containing TV and VCR, plus extras like robes, hair dryers and fresh flowers. The Wilson Room is the largest with fireplace, queen-size bed, whirlpool tub and separate shower. The room's colours are turquoise, pink and yellow and its sitting area has large windows overlooking the harbour. The Copper Room also overlooks the water and has a queen bed with floral duvets, plus a desk. Another, the Quarry Room, has twin beds and is the only one without a harbour view. These are all on the second floor. On the first, you'll find the wheelchair-accessible Salter Room which is decorated around a fly-fishing theme. Perfect for business travellers, it has a desk and phone, plus fax and computer access.

I don't know about you, but I can hardly wait to visit.

The Willows

On the north shore of Lake Superior, this B&B makes for memorable stopover between Sault Ste. Marie and Thunder Bay.

Brockwell Chambers

Maria Sutton
183 Brock St.
Sault Ste. Marie, ON P6A 3B8
705-949-1076

Best time to call: anytime
Season: all year
Rates: S $65-85, D $75-95 (plus GST)
Restrictions: no children, no smoking, no guests' pets
Facilities: 3 bedrooms (1 twin-bedded, 1 double, 1 king); 3 en suite bathrooms (1 shower/Jacuzzi tub, 1 shower/tub, 1 shower only); living room and verandah for guests; telephone in room; computer, fax on request
Parking: off-street for up to 5 cars
Breakfast: full
Location: downtown Sault Ste. Marie, handy to International Bridge and I-75
Directions: from E or N, take Hwy 17B, then follow "Bridge to USA" signs along Wellington St. E to Brock St. From S, follow "To Hwy 17" signs and turn left on Brock St.

Every ounce the gracious host (she even dresses the part), Maria Sutton welcomes you into the grand entrance hall of Brockwell Chambers B&B. With rich red broadloom underfoot, she leads you up the wide stairs to the guest bedrooms. All are large, with polished hardwood floors and shiny new en suite bathrooms. All contain TVs, VCRs, radios, tape decks, and telephones. And *all* are beautifully deco-rated. The Yellow and Pink Rooms are the largest and both have fireplaces and king-size beds, though the Pink is usually made up as a twin. The smaller Blue Room has a double bed and its bathroom has a shower only.

Maria, and husband Roy, have owned this early 1900s brick mansion for a few years now. It was subdivided and down-at-heels when they bought but over the years they've restored it back to the way it was originally. Luckily, most of the significant architectural features were still intact, though hidden behind dividing walls and dropped ceilings.

Next morning, you'll have breakfast in the beamed dining room set up with several tables for guests. We were the only ones there, so Maria placed us at a smaller table set with white linens and Rosenthal china. Fruit cocktail was set out when we came downstairs and we helped ourselves to tea and cereal from the sideboard. My companion had bacon and eggs and I had waffles.

After, we took our tea into the living room, but you may well end up out on the verandah with its comfortable rattan furniture. It's a pleasant way to get your day organized before starting out.

200

— Brackwell Chambers B&B —

A restored mansion convenient to downtown and good restaurants.

Top o' the Hill

Margaret and Bernt Brauer
40 Broos Road
Sault-Ste-Marie, ON P6C 5S4
705-253-9041
Fax: 705-946-5571
E-mail: brauerb@sympatico.ca

Best time to call: anytime
Besides English: German
Season: May to Oct
Rates: S $45, D $65-95 (no taxes)
Restrictions: no smoking, no guests' pets
Facilities: 3 bedrooms (1 king, 1 queen, 1 twin); 2 bathrooms (1 shower/tub, shared, 1 shower only en suite); guest living room
Parking: plenty on site
Breakfast: full 7:15-9:00 AM, continental before and after
Location: a 12-minute drive from downtown
Directions: follow signs to airport until Second Line West (Hwy 550). From Second Line and Hwy 17N, go 7.5 kms on Second Line to Broos Rd. Turn right and you'll see Top o' the Hill

I found out about Top o' the Hill in a letter from the host herself. Margaret Brauer wrote that their home was set into a hill on the outskirts of town, and that it was designed for their large family, now grown. She'd redecorated and opened as a B&B. From the photos, it reminded me of a villa, surrounded by gardens.

It's quite a jaunt from my home in Port Hope to Sault Ste. Marie and I was *not* looking forward to the 700-kilometre drive. But it turned out to be worth it. Margaret and husband Bernt proved to be superb hosts and though the house is distinctly modern, the three bedrooms are distinctly not – they're a mix of Victorian and country.

All three bedrooms are upstairs. The Garden Room has a king-size bed, en suite bath and private balcony. Here, blue and white Laura Ashley linens complement the Brauers' collection of Delft china. Large and bright, its window overlooks the gardens and city beyond. The Victorian Room has a Circassian walnut bedroom suite with queen-size bed, a 10th-birthday gift to Margaret's mother in 1915. The twin-bedded Amish Room has more of a country feel. These last two share a bathroom, with shower, down the hall.

The printed breakfast menu offers a choice, and even asks about special dietary needs. I had waffles (outstanding) and blueberries with St. Joe's Island maple syrup. After, you won't lack for things to do and see. As well as attractions like the Agawa Canyon, famous for its fall colours, there are some fascinating spots just across the border. Like Mackinac Island, an hour's drive away. Loaded with mansions, it's a sure pick for "Lifestyles of the Rich and Famous."

— Top o' the Hill —

Though the house is distinctly modern, the rooms are distinctly turn-of-the-century.

203

The Golden Apple Bed & Breakfast

Carol Blasdale and
Arlene McDermott
78 Bruce St.
Thornbury, ON N0H 2P0
519-599-3850 (Fax 599-7751)

Best time to call: 9 AM – 9 PM
Season: all year
Rates: S $55, D $70 (no taxes)
Restrictions: no children,
smoking outside, no guests' pets
Facilities: 3 bedrooms (1 twin-
bedded, 2 queen); 2 bathrooms
(1 shower/tub, 1 2 pce down-
stairs) parlour and reading room
for guests; ceiling fans in
bedrooms; telephones in halls;
fax at cost
Parking: off-street for 6 cars
Breakfast: full
In residence: Gertie, the cat
Location: Thornbury is 2 hrs N of
Toronto on Georgian Bay
Directions: drive N on Hwy 400
to Barrie, then W on Hwy 26,
through Collingwood. Go
another 20 kms to Thornbury.
Turn left at Bruce St stoplights

Sisters Carol Blasdale and Arlene
McDermott, with families grown, decided
to leave big cities (Toronto and Winnipeg
respectively) to run a B&B. Thornbury's
Golden Apple was up for sale and was, it
turned out, perfect for their needs. Not lost
on the sisters was the fact that they could
both have access to the many sports they
enjoyed: tennis, hiking, cycling, sailing,
downhill and cross-country skiing. (And if
they ever decide to take up golf, there are
four courses within a 20-minute drive.)   In
no time they'd moved in and were redeco-
rating.

Inside, the decor is genteel and restful –
from the parlour and reading room downstairs to the three guest bedrooms upstairs.
At the top of the stairs, the cosy Blue Room
has twin beds and lace curtains on its
windows. Around the corner, the queen-
bedded Yellow Room is traditionally
furnished and right across the hall from the
bathroom.   The largest bedroom, but
furthest from the shared bathroom, is the

Turret Room with queen-size bed and
stained glass windows.

I found several art books in my room
and had a fascinating read about the
Canadian architect-designed Musee
D'Orsay in Paris. Turns out Arlene's the
one with the keen interest – as a Winnipeg
Art Gallery volunteer, she escorted various
art tours to Europe. She says she tries to
deduce what guests might like to read, so
the little "library" in each room changes
regularly.

Next morning, I had breakfast in the
Victorian dining room papered in a dusty
rose moiré. Arlene and Carol typically serve
fruit (including a warm pear comport made
with pears from their own garden), buttermilk scones or apple muffins, followed by
something like wild-blueberry pancakes or
orange French toast. And, oh yes, to be
expected from this sporty pair, their own
homemade health food cereal.